REVOLUTION

EVERYDAY EVANGELISM
TO ROCK YOUR CAMPUS

JAY STRACK

NELSON IMPACT
A Division of Thomas Nelson Publishers
Since 1798

www.thomasnelson.com

Published by Nelson Impact, a Division of Thomas Nelson, Inc., P.O. Box 141000, Nashville, TN 37214.

ISBN 1-4185-0595-1

Printed in the United States of America

06 07 08 09 RRD 9 8 7 6 5 4 3 2 1

Page design by Crosslin Creative
2743 Douglas Lane, Thompsons Station, Tennessee 37179

CONTENTS

INTRODUCTION 5

KEY. 7

THE ROMAN ROAD TO SALVATION. 9

1. IT STARTS WITH YOU!. 13

2. THE MANDATE FROM ABOVE 31

3. MIRACLE WITHIN 47

4. MOTIVATED BY THE MULTITUDES 65

5. PRAYING FOR THE LOST 79

6. THE MOUNTAIN BEHIND US 97

7. THE MEETING AHEAD, PART 1 115

8. THE MEETING AHEAD, PART 2 129

"I BELIEVE IN PRAYER" JOURNAL 147

NOTES. 148

ABOUT THE AUTHOR 151

INTRODUCTION

The Bible tells the history of mankind—the ebb and flow of life, the fame and failures, the triumphs and tragedies. Within its pages are stories of powerful revolutions; positive, God-revolutions that empower, change, and move man forward to new choices and right living.

And the an important part of each of God's revolutions has been the power of one person:

✦ When the people did evil in the sight of the Lord, He called Deborah and she led the people to willingly serve the Lord. (Check out Judges 4-5.)

✦ In 1 Samuel 13 and 14, we read that the Lord sought for Himself a man *after His own heart,*

and David stepped forward.

✦ The Lord said to Ezekiel in time of great drought and barrenness in the land that He sought for a man *to stand the gap* (Ezekiel 22:30).

✦ To *prepare the way* for the greatest revolution in the history of the planet—the arrival of the Messiah, the Son of God—God sent forth a man named John the Baptist (Mark 1:3).

There are many others, but each one who has been used of God to bring about a revolution had several common characteristics as seen in 2 Chronicles 16:9: "For the eyes of the Lord run to and fro throughout the whole earth, to show Himself strong on behalf of those whose heart is loyal to Him." God is looking for those whom He can use. He is on the lookout for a heart that is:

1. Loyal. A heart that is devoted completely to Him. No locked doors, nothing swept under the rug, nothing hidden. A heart that is the same on Saturday night as it is on Sunday morning.

2. Full of integrity. A heart that is faithfully honest, even when no one else is looking.

3. Enthusiastic. Literally, a heart that is *en Theos* (in God), and one that is consumed. As the Russian poet Boris Pasternak said: "it is . . . someone's soul inspired and ablaze" that clears the road to new and better days.

Using the model of the ultimate revolutionary—the apostle Paul—a man who shook the world for Christ, as well as examples of students just like you, the lessons in this study guide will teach you how to impact your campus, your youth group, and your family as a devoted follower of Christ. Get ready to experience the collision of purpose and passion in your life and the ignition it creates in the lives of others!

KEY

STUDENT LEADERSHIP UNIVERSITY CURRICULUM

Throughout this study guide, you will see several icons or headings that represent an idea, a statement, or a question that we want you to consider as you experience Scripture in this study guide series. Refer to the descriptions below to help you remember what the icons and headings mean.

transfuse (trans FYOOZ) ; to cause to pass from one to another; transmit

The goal of the lesson for the week.

Experience Scripture: Learning to really experience Scripture is the key element to "getting" who God is and all that He has in store for you.

infuse (in FYOOZ) ; to cause to be permeated with something (as a principle or quality) that alters usually for the better

Through journaling, group discussion, and personal study, experience Scripture as it permeates your heart and alters your life.

Future Tense Living: Your choices today will determine your future. Learn how to live with dynamic purpose and influence.

Attitude Reloaded: Rethink your attitude! Learn to replace self-centered, negative, or limited thoughts with positive, courageous, compassionate thoughts that are based on God's unlimited ability and power.

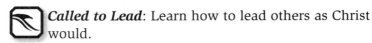 ***In His Steps:*** Every attitude and action of your life should begin with the questions, How would Jesus respond to this person and situation before me? What would He choose to do?

diffuse (di FYOOZ) : to pour out and permit or cause to spread freely; to extend, scatter

Once God's Word is infused into your heart, it will pour forth to others without restraint. In this section, explore what that looks like in your daily life.

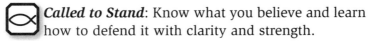 ***Called to Lead***: Learn how to lead others as Christ would.

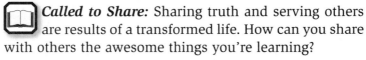 ***Called to Stand***: Know what you believe and learn how to defend it with clarity and strength.

Called to Share: Sharing truth and serving others are results of a transformed life. How can you share with others the awesome things you're learning?

One Thing: Consider ONE THING you can do this week to make a difference in your life and/or the life of another.

FUSE BOX

Power up for the week with this focused truth.

THE ROMAN ROAD TO SALVATION

Keep it Simple! This Gospel presentation is powerful and effective, and has worked in the lives of students at the beach, in the locker room, on the street, or one-on-one with a friend. If you care enough to share, you will be used of God to lead someone to life-changing salvation in Christ.

Go to Romans in your Bible or pocket New Testament. Highlight the following verses:

1. Romans 3:23, " . . . *for all have sinned and fall short of the glory of God . . . "*

Everyone has sinned and will sin – *all of us.*

> It doesn't help to measure "little" sins or "not as bad as others."

Everyone *falls short of the glory of God.*
> The only standard of measurement is God – He is holy and man isn't. That means a barrier, no matter the size, is in the way between you and God.

2. Romans 5:8, *"But God demonstrates His own love toward us, in that while we were still sinners, Christ died for us."*

> We've got a problem–sin. He has the answer.

> He chose to love us and pay the price for our sin. When He cried out "it is finished" on the cross, He let the world know that our sins are now "paid in full." This solves the problem of the sin barrier between us and God–only Christ can remove it.

3. Romans 6:23, *"For the wages of sin is death, but the gift of God is eternal life in Christ Jesus our Lord."*

The wages or payment of sin is death,
> **BUT** *the gift of God* is eternal life!

We don't deserve it, can't earn it, but must receive it.

Salvation is a *gift*, no strings attached.

Everyone has a gift waiting—it's got your name on it, and it's ready for you to open.

4. Romans 10:9, "*. . . that if you confess with your mouth the Lord Jesus and believe in your heart that God has raised Him from the dead, you will be saved.*"

Sounds too easy, huh? Just say that Jesus is Lord?

Well, actually, that is **a lot to say!**

To *confess is to agree with God* that Jesus is the risen Savior Who died for your sins.

There is no other way to salvation other than the gift He paid and the victory over sin that only Christ could perform; that is, a resurrection from the dead.

With your mouth involves a declaration of the mind and,

believe in your heart involves a genuine, life-transforming *faith* that He is *Lord!*

Lord means that He is the ruler of all, and by making this statement, you are asking Him to be ruler of your heart and life.

5. Romans 10:13, "*whoever calls on the name of the Lord shall be saved.*"

Now that you understand the need and the solution, it is up to you to simply *call on the name of the Lord.*

Note: Salvation is for everyone – for *whoever calls.* Salvation is definite–you *shall be saved,* not "might" be, but *will* be.

Here is a simple *call* through prayer:

Dear Lord Jesus,
    I want to thank you for loving me and for dying on the cross for all of my sins and mistakes.

I have hurt others, I have hurt myself, and I have hurt You. Thank You for sparing my life so that I might hear of your love, your death on the cross, and your resurrection. I understand that this resurrection means that every sin that I have committed has been paid for and forgiven.

The best I know how, I ask you to forgive my sin and I call upon your name to receive this gift of eternal life. I believe in my heart that You are Lord and ask you to be Lord of my life.

Thank you for listening and for answering my prayer. Help me know to grow in my faith as I trust you and to obey all that I read in your word. I pray this in your name. Amen.

This prayer is not magic. But it is taken from verses in the Word of God that teach us how to receive eternal life. It is a genuine *call* to Christ to be Savior and Lord, whether you pray all of it or a form of it as you read through the verses. Christ looks upon the heart, listens to the mind, and hears the mouth–He knows what you are asking, even as you might struggle to ask it.

Trust Him today and begin a new life.

CHAPTER 1

IT STARTS WITH YOU!

KEY SCRIPTURE

Go therefore and make disciples of all the nations, baptizing them in the name of the Father and of the Son and of the Holy Spirit, teaching them to observe all things that I have commanded you; and lo, I am with you always, even to the end of the age. Amen.
—**Matthew 28:19–20**

THIS REALLY HAPPENED!

Evangelist Rick Stanley tells a remarkable story about growing up as Elvis Presley's younger stepbrother. Even though there were celebrities and parties every day in his life, Rick still could not find peace.

Rick kept asking out Robin, a pretty blonde girl who was different from everyone else he knew. She continually turned him down because she had made a commitment to date only Christians, and Rick was as far from God as you could be. Every time he approached Robin, she told Rick that she was praying for him and shared the gospel of Christ with him.

Rick thought Robin's faith was silly, but he was intrigued with her different spirit. Throughout high school, the two were friends. Rick occasionally tried to get her to come to celebrity parties at Elvis's mansion, but Robin was not impressed.

While Robin lived for Christ, Rick drifted into drugs and the party life. He traveled with Elvis and met many starlets and Playboy bunnies. These girls filled the mansion almost every night. Yet the one person Rick could not get out of his mind was the fifteen-year-old bubbly, pure-hearted blonde with braces who said, "I'm praying for you" every time he saw her.

A few years later, empty and broken, Rick called Robin to ask her how to find peace. After three years of friendship and praying for him, she led Rick to personal faith in Christ. He told her later that it was her consistent testimony of joy and peace that made him want to know the Lord and leave behind his old life. In fact, he was so grateful and cared for her so much that he married her!

WHY KNOW IT?

✦ Two out of three born-again Christians (64%) accept Jesus Christ as their Savior before their eighteenth birthday.[1]

✦ One out of eight born-again people (13%) made their profession of faith while eighteen to twenty-one years old.[2]

transfuse (trans FYOOZ): to cause to pass from one to another; transmit

Campus revolution starts with you—or rather, with Christ *in* you.

You may have heard of the phenomenon called an *artesian well*, a deep well that taps into a natural water source and constantly floods fresh water outward or up-ward. It is not to be mistaken for a still well of water; it is not a stream. This is an active, flowing water source.

Those of us who know Christ have an active artesian well in our hearts. Jesus referred to it as the *abundant life*. He said, "I have come that they may have life, and that they may have it more abundantly" (John 10:10).

Whoever drinks of the water that I shall give him will never thirst. But the water that I shall give him will become in him a fountain of water springing up into everlasting life. —**John 4:14**

If anyone thirsts, let him come to Me and drink. He who believes in Me, as the Scripture has said, out of his heart will flow rivers of living water. —**John 7:37–38**

Jesus said that once we have experienced the miracle of abundant life, we will have "rivers of living water" springing up inside us. Personal evangelism naturally happens as the well inside our hearts abundantly floods out to others so that they can also partake and enjoy the fullness of Christ's love.

It sounds easy. So why don't we do it?

What has happened to that flow of living water?

infuse (in FYOOZ): to cause to be permeated with something (as a principle or quality) that alters usually for the better

Why Don't We Share God's Love?

There are several reasons that might explain why you and other students do not share the love of God with others.

   1. You have never met Christ personally. You might know *about* Him, but you do not *know* Him.

The bottom line is this: when you personally receive Christ, you have been given the power to become a son or daughter of God. "As many as received Him, to them

He gave the right to become children of God, to those who believe in His name" (John 1:12).

The Greek could be translated in this verse: "you have been given supernatural power." Supernatural, not superhero! This means that God has stepped out of heaven and come into your heart. You experience His transforming power on a daily basis.

Jesus told Nicodemus, a very religious and morally pure man, that he must be "born of the spirit" (John 3:8). He went on to say that God loved him so much that if he would believe in Jesus, he would have "everlasting life" (v. 16).

ASK YOURSELF

Have you been "born of the spirit"? Are you *in Christ* or only *near Him?*

2. You have willful sin in your life.

Sometimes a well no longer flows because it is stopped up. There are habits and thoughts that are clogging the water source and ruling your heart. You might be hanging out with people or at places that contribute to the clog.

3. You are *in Christ,* but far from Him.

Living for Christ has become a yawn, routine, and some days even optional. Because your quiet time is weak, the debris of the culture's media and message has more control in your heart and mind than the Word of God.

4. You don't know how to share your faith (or *think* you don't know how).

Although a person could learn many ways to intelligently discuss world religions or debate the existence of God intellectually, all you really need to do is simply tell your own story of how Christ transformed your life.

What about you? If Jesus is not a big deal in your life, if He doesn't totally amaze you, fill you, and transform every area of what you think and do with His majesty and intense love for you, then it is time to find out what's stopping up the flow.

THINK ABOUT IT

When and how did you give your life to Christ, and how has that choice affected you?

If you were walking down the halls and you saw a student on the floor, pale and ill, obviously in desperate need of water, what would you do?

+ Keep walking because it's none of your business.

+ Don't stop because he might not like the water you give him, or he might laugh at the cup you give it to him in.

+ Casually stroll by because he once criticized you.

No! You wouldn't do any of that. You would run as fast as you could to the nearest water source and get that person some water. Without hesitation, you would see the person's need and meet that need.

Choose which of the above three options you might be and write it below:

_____

_____

_____

My life most closely represents # _____ because

_____

_____

_____

With Christ, a heart can be changed in a moment through surrender to God's will and confession of sin. Now it's time to clean out the well in your heart and get it flowing again.

diffuse (di FYOOZ) : to pour out and permit or cause to spread freely; to extend, scatter

The Bible tells us that Isaac faced two famines in his life. One famine occurred in the days of his father, Abraham; and one he faced alone (Genesis 26:1).

What Causes a Famine?

1. Heaven is silent and there is a lack of rain.

> *Take heed to yourselves, lest your heart be deceived, and you turn aside and serve other gods and worship them, lest the Lord's anger be aroused against you, and He shut up the heavens so that there be no rain.* —**Deuteronomy 11:16–17**

There are recorded times in history when, because of people's sin and rebellion, God simply shut up the heavens and there was no rain. When God's people turn their back on Him through willful sin, He must withhold His blessings during that time.

2. The enemy would cut off the water supply by stopping up the wells with debris.

Now the Philistines had stopped up all the wells which his father's servants had dug in the days of Abraham his father, and they had filled them with earth. —**Genesis 26:15**

Abraham and Isaac experienced several ways in which the enemy stopped up their wells. These are like the ways the wellspring of joy from a Christian is sometimes stopped up, causing him or her not to share the love of God with others.

✦ *The well was filled with decaying flesh of dead animals that contaminated the water.* Satan uses the lust of the flesh to urge us into sin that contaminates and destroys our testimony to others. We must never forget that we have an enemy of our souls who wants to stop up the well of living water that flows in our life.

> If you have willful rebellion against God in your heart, God cannot bless you; and, as a result, you cannot bless others. In effect, *others* experience *your* famine.

✦ *The well was filled up with dirt so that water could not flow.* This was not outright contamination but dirt that blocked the flow. Similarly, dirt in our life—such as language, hidden sin, and sexual immorality—blocks our fellowship to God.

◆ *Because water was the most valuable commodity in the desert, the enemy would even consider using gold, silk fabrics, or precious metals to stop up the well.* These precious metals represent the blessings of God, the good things in our lives, that can sometimes distract us from God and stop up our wellspring of living water.

Most student surveys reveal that we pray the least when things are going the best—when we made the team, things are good at home, we have good friendships, and things are going well for us. We become so content that we forget about those around us who are still thirsty for life. We stop sharing and hoard the water to ourselves.

What about you? Do you pray more or less often when things are going well?

_____

_____

_____

Dig the Wells Again

> *And Isaac dug again the wells of water which they had dug in the days of Abraham his father, for the Philistines had stopped them up after the death of Abraham. He called them by the names which his father had called them.* —**Genesis 26:18**

Some commentators suggest Isaac knew what to do during the second famine because he had already experienced a similar crisis with his father. As a child, he had watched his father dig the wells so their family could survive during a famine.

Isaac knew that the only way to get the water to flow again was to get on your knees and start cleaning out the debris. Once the wells were dug again, Isaac probably was among the first to taste the fresh, life-giving water.

 You can't share the water of life if your well is shut down. So what should you do?

✦ *Get on your knees:* Begin with a humble spirit and say, "Lord, I *want* to clean out the well of my heart."

✦ *Identify the debris:* Your self-inspection is backed up by a Holy Spirit conviction. There are sins of *commission* (what you do) and sins of *omission* (what you should do but don't do). In light of this, consider your behaviors and tendencies in the following areas:

> If we confess our sins, He is faithful and just to forgive us our sins and to cleanse us from all unrighteousness.
> —1 John 1:9

➤ stuff I see on the Internet

➤ friends I hang out with

➤ movies I go to see

➤ the quality of my quiet time

➤ thoughts I play with

➤ sexual stuff

➤ relationship with my parents

➤ my general spirit

✦ *Clean out the well.* Confess your sin to God, and allow the Holy Spirit to work in your heart to remove the debris.

There Is a Famine in Our Land

Why do you suppose a young person would commit date rape, become an alcoholic, experiment with homosexuality, or participate in sexual activity? Why would a student open fire on his schoolmates or strap a bomb to his body and blow up innocent people, including children?

There is a spiritual famine in the land because the wells of many Christians are stopped up, and the water of life is not shared with others.

The Bedouins of Israel still live in tents in the desert, much as Abraham and Isaac lived. If you had the opportunity to visit them, they might share with you an old saying that still applies today: "The great sin of the desert is to know where there is water and not share it."

+ What happens when you make the team? Do you keep it to yourself or tell people?

+ What about when you get a good grade on a test or paper? Do you tell anyone?

+ What if you get a date to homecoming, find a new job, or meet someone interesting? Do you keep quiet?

Whenever good news happens, it is natural to want to share it, tell it, and enjoy it with others. When you have Christ in your life and you see others in a famine, you can't help but want to say, "Here is water." This is our call in Christ: to share the good news.

THINK ABOUT IT

You belong to a youth group with Christian friends who know the truth, who are surrounded by the truth. They probably go to youth camp, on mission trips, to Christian concerts, and hear the Bible taught regularly. Consider:

◆ How many teens have been led to Christ through your youth group?

◆ How many have been impacted by your class?

◆ How many want to know Christ because of your testimony?

What is ONE THING you can share with a person you see every day at school?

◆ "God loves you just as you are, but He loves you too much to leave you that way."

◆ "I'm praying for you."

◆ "God has a unique plan for your life."

◆ Other: _____

_____

ASK YOURSELF

Why does it take a school shooting, a teen suicide, or the death of a friend for us to shed tears and begin to care?

How many nights will we go to bed dry-eyed when so many in our school cry themselves to sleep?

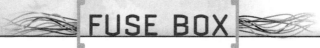

FUSE BOX

Those of us who have the water of life cannot keep it to ourselves. The only remedy for the spiritual famine of this generation is genuine salvation.

NOTES

He leads us to lead others to Himself.
—John Maxwell

PRIVATE WORLD DEVOTIONS

MONDAY: See it. Read the surrounding passages or chapter for the Key Scripture so that you can get an understanding of the background and context. This helps you to really *see* the verse.

TUESDAY: Hear it. Read the daily Key Scripture and/or surrounding passage out loud, putting your name in, if applicable. For example, John *can do all things through Christ. Thieves have come to destroy* John, *but Jesus has come that* John *might have eternal life.*

WEDNESDAY: Write it. Write the verse and then what it says about:

+ *Others:* Respond, serve, and love as Jesus would.
+ *Me:* Specific attitudes, choices, or habits.
+ *God:* His love, mercy, holiness, peace, joy, etc.

PRIVATE WORLD JOURNAL

*I am grateful for—I praise You for—I am
feeling—I am thinking—I need help with*

PRIVATE WORLD DEVOTIONS *(Continued)*

THURSDAY: Memorize it. Take the verse with you—write it on a card or put it in your phone, iPod, or PDA. Go over it throughout the day so that it begins to *live* in your heart and mind.

FRIDAY: Pray it. Personalize the verse as you pray for yourself or for others or in praise to God. To pray is literally "to think about." Try thinking out loud or writing in your **PRIVATE WORLD JOURNAL**.

SATURDAY: Share it. Ask the Lord to bring someone to mind or in your path today who needs good news. Don't be shy—just let it out! Whether you IM, write, text, tell, or send it, the joy of God's Word will flow from your heart into theirs.

PRAYER REQUESTS

Date	Name	Need	Answer

PRIVATE WORLD JOURNAL

I am grateful for—I praise You for—I am feeling—I am thinking—I need help with

NOTES

CHAPTER 2

THE MANDATE FROM ABOVE

KEY SCRIPTURE

Paul, a bondservant of Jesus Christ, called to be an apostle, separated to the gospel of God which He promised before through His prophets in the Holy Scriptures, concerning His Son Jesus Christ our Lord, who was born of the seed of David according to the flesh, and declared to be the Son of God with power according to the Spirit of holiness, by the resurrection from the dead.

—Romans 1:1–4

THIS REALLY HAPPENED!

Brent never missed a church service, but it wasn't because he wanted to be there. His dad was the pastor, and the rule at home was church every Sunday—no exceptions.

He doesn't remember exactly when it happened, but he knows that he got sidetracked in life and began to try alcohol and the party life in his teens. At first, it seemed like no big deal to drink on a Friday night, but then he noticed that his attitude changed. He fought with his parents more often and cared less and less about school.

This went on for a few years. Brent remembers the night, one Sunday in church, when he got there early and sat in the empty church alone. People started to come in and the service started, but he never noticed. That was the night God grabbed his heart and shook it.

Brent says he will never forget God speaking to his heart, saying, "Why are you wasting your life? There is so much you can do for Me!"

During the invitation, he walked forward, where he presented himself to his dad. "God has called me to preach," Brent announced. His dad was shocked.

But it was true. Brent had received a mandate from God, and he was obedient to the heavenly vision to preach the good news. He began immediately to do so and then went on to seminary to obtain two master's degrees: one in theology and one in ethics. Today, God is using Brent Crowe to present the Word of God to thousands of students across the country.

WHY KNOW IT?

✦ "The Establishment Clause of the First Amendment does not prohibit purely private religious speech by students."[1]

✦ "Students therefore have the same right to engage in individual or group prayer and religious discussion during the school day as they do to engage in other comparable activity. For example, students may read their Bibles or other scriptures, say grace before meals, and pray before tests to the same extent they may engage in comparable nondisruptive activities."[2]

✦ "Students in informal settings, such as cafeterias and hallways, may pray and discuss their religious views with each other, subject to the same rules of order as apply to other student activities and speech. Students may also speak to, and attempt to persuade, their peers about religious topics just as they do with regard to political topics. School officials, however, should intercede to stop student speech that constitutes harassment aimed at a student or a group of students."[3]

+ "Students may also participate in before or after school events with religious content on the same terms as they may participate in other extra-curriculum activities on school premises. School officials may neither discourage nor encourage participation in such an event."[4]

+ The Equal Access Act is designed to ensure that, consistent with the First Amendment, student religious activities are accorded the same access to public school facilities as are student secular activities.[5]

transfuse (trans FYOOZ): to cause to pass from one to another; transmit

It has been stated, and rightly so, that vision is the single greatest leadership trait one can possess. To be more precise, *obedience to the heavenly vision* is of even more value and importance.

In Acts 26, the apostle Paul fulfills his destiny as he stands before King Agrippa and the governor. He asks for permission to speak, and chooses to preach the gospel by sharing his personal testimony.

So I said, "Who are You, Lord?" And He said, "I am Jesus, whom you are persecuting. But rise and stand on your feet; for I have appeared to you for this purpose, to make you a minister and a witness both of the things which you have seen and of the things which I will yet reveal to you. I will deliver you from the Jewish people, as well as from the Gentiles, to whom I now send you, to open their eyes, in order to turn them from darkness to light, and from the power of

Satan to God, that they may receive forgiveness of sins and an inheritance among those who are sanctified by faith in Me." Therefore, King Agrippa, I was not disobedient to the heavenly vision, but declared . . . that the Christ would suffer, that He would be the first to rise from the dead, and would proclaim light to the Jewish people and to the Gentiles. —Acts 26:15–19, 23

infuse (in FYOOZ)'; to cause to be permeated with something (as a principle or quality) that alters usually for the better

With great confidence and passion, Paul gives a dissertation about the transformation that only Jesus Christ can make. He tells the complete gospel—that is, that "Christ would suffer, that He would be the first to rise from the dead" (v. 23).

Paul knew that he had little time to speak, so he went right for the presentation of the gospel: Christ suffered and died on the cross and then was resurrected from the dead. He knew that this might be the only opportunity he had to share the gospel with these men, and it might be the only chance they ever had to hear it.

 Suppose that this week you have one chance to tell the good news to a crowd at your school.

Would you do it?

❑ Yes

❑ No

Could you do it?

❑ Yes

❑ No

If the opportunity presents itself this week, will you have the boldness and courage to speak up?

❏ Yes

❏ No

It didn't matter that he was on trial for his life. Paul chose to seize the day and to take advantage of the opportunity to speak up for Christ.

What robs you of the courage to present the gospel?

What can you do to change your attitude or your circumstances?

The apostle Paul was not about to be stopped by:

✦ *anything*—the possibility of beatings or even death

✦ or *anyone*—the intimidation of the powerful rulers before him or the spectators waiting nearby to laugh at him.

diffuse (di FYOOZ)'; to pour out and permit or cause to spread freely; to extend, scatter

With confidence, Paul boldly speaks freely once again by exalting Jesus and describing his divine call. He tells King Agrippa, "I was not disobedient to the heavenly vision" (v. 19).

There are two important things that Paul wants these men of the government to know:

1. His mandate to preach was ordered from above by the One whose power is higher than theirs.

2. His message is a divine vision of a Savior who suffered for man and then rose from the dead in victory so that anyone who believes can be saved.

The Message from Above

It was the genuineness of his heavenly vision that strengthened Paul to speak boldly regardless of the possible consequences, even the taking of his life.

Paul may have had concern about his life when he presented the gospel, but you probably do not have to be concerned about whether you'll lose your life for sharing Christ at your school. Unlike the apostle Paul, in this country you are protected by the government and have the freedom to talk about Jesus Christ and to carry your Bible.[6]

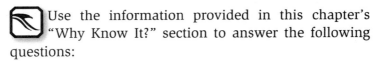 Use the information provided in this chapter's "Why Know It?" section to answer the following questions:

✦ Is there anything legally that would stop you from starting a Christian club on campus or a Bible study at your school?

✦ According to the information from the U.S. Department of Education, can you legally carry a Bible to school or wear a Christian T-shirt?

✦ Are you allowed to invite people from your school to your church?

If these things are permissible legally, then what is holding you back from being a spiritual leader on campus?

Check out www.studentz.com for info and ideas from various national ministries on how to make a difference on your campus.

What is the ONE THING you can begin to do this week as an action step toward getting a group together on your campus?

- ✦ Contact a school counselor.

- ✦ Talk to your youth pastor.

- ✦ Research info on the Web.

- ✦ Talk to friends about it.

GROUP DISCUSSION

Discuss with your group or class which of the statements in the "Why Know It?" section is most helpful to you in being successful as a spiritual leader at your school.

Be sure that you clearly understand the gospel message from above so that you can tell it to others as Paul did: " . . . that the Christ would suffer, that He would be the first to rise from the dead, and would proclaim light to the Jewish people and to the Gentiles" (Acts 26:23).

The word *gospel* means good news; in fact, this news is so good that it seems too good to be true when we first hear the amazing story of God's love, forgiveness, and sacrifice.

The Messenger

This message is delivered by Paul, who describes himself as a "bondservant" and an "apostle" (Romans 1:1). Let's take a closer look at each of these descriptions.

Bondservant. Imagine—one of history's greatest leaders and authors introduces himself as a "bondservant." This was not a flattering term in the society, for bondservants were the lowest of classes; but to Paul, it was a privileged title.

The word *servant* is from the Greek word that means "to bind." King Agrippa would have understood this language:

✦ A bondservant is one who is bound to another in slavery by birth. Paul is saying that he has been born again into a spiritual bondage to serve Christ, but this "bondage" is something he holds as a privilege and a joy.

✦ The union between a bondservant and his master could only be broken through death; it was permanent, just as we are joined to Christ for eternity.

✦ *Bondservant* refers to "one whose will is swallowed up in the will of another."[7]

Paul was a Jew, and it is also possible that he had in mind the Hebrew slave of ancient days. The slave loved the master and his family so much that he often returned to them after being set free and volunteered himself for a lifetime of bondage.

Apostle. Paul also calls himself an "apostle," which means "one who is sent." Who sent Paul? It is clear that God did.

The Greek word for *apostle* is conveyed in English as "missionary." Paul had the privilege of being designated as a missionary who devoted his life to sharing the good news of Jesus Christ around the world.

 Paul's bold courage to speak boldly about Christ to the king came from two things:

1. *His personal transformation through Christ.* Have you been transformed?

2. *His understanding of who he was in Christ: a bondservant and an apostle.* Who are you? Are you a courageous Christian with a heavenly call or a student who struggles to live for Christ?

> *Paul, a bondservant of Jesus Christ,*
> *called to be an apostle, separated to*
> *the gospel of God which He promised*
> *before through His prophets in*
> *the Holy Scriptures, concerning*
> *His Son Jesus Christ our Lord, who*
> *was born of the seed of David according*
> *to the flesh, and declared to be the Son*
> *of God with power according to the*
> *Spirit of holiness, by the resurrection*
> *from the dead.* —**Romans 1:1–4**

In these verses, Paul says that the good news—this heavenly message that must be shared with everyone on the planet—is threefold:

1. *Jesus is the revealed One promised in the Old Testament* (v. 2). He is the One who has come to fulfill the prophecies. He is the sent One, the anointed One; He is the long-awaited Messiah.

The book of Revelation calls Jesus "the Alpha and the Omega, the first and the last" (22:13). That means He is the first word and the last word on all the decisions and issues of your life.

2. *Jesus is the reigning One, the seed of David* (v. 3). He is the Lord, the One to whom "every knee should bow" and "every tongue should confess" (Philippians 2:10–11).

3. *Jesus is the resurrected One who paid it all* (v. 4). The fact that He rose from the dead is proof that we are free from the power of sin, the penalty of sin, and the presence of sin.

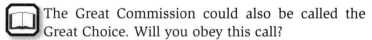 Because this is a heavenly message, each of us who has experienced Jesus, who died and rose again, lives a life "on call." You are on assignment, mandated by heaven, and should have a heart that is ready and available at all times. When walking up and down the halls of your school, you must remember this heavenly mandate and not be deterred by the culture.

The Heavenly Call

Just before Jesus ascended back to heaven, He gave His disciples what is often called the Great Commission: "Go therefore and make disciples of all the nations, baptizing them in the name of the Father and of the Son and of the Holy Spirit, teaching them to observe all things that I have commanded you; and lo, I am with you always, even to the end of the age" (Matthew 28:19–20).

The Great Commission could also be called the Great Choice. Will you obey this call?

This vision, when obeyed, will give you

✦ the conviction to stand

✦ the confidence to speak

✦ the compassion to share

✦ the courage to put others first

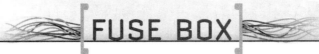

[FUSE BOX]

It is commendable and scriptural that you go on mission trips. But if you only share the gospel on designated mission trips and not in your everyday life, then you are not fulfilling the Great Commission.

The great doors of opportunity swing open on the tiny hinges of obedience.
—Dr. Ike Reighard

PRIVATE WORLD DEVOTIONS

MONDAY: See it. Read the surrounding passages or chapter for the Key Scripture so that you can get an understanding of the background and context. This helps you to really *see* the verse.

TUESDAY: Hear it. Read the daily Key Scripture and/or surrounding passage out loud, putting your name in, if applicable. For example, <u>John</u> *can do all things through Christ. Thieves have come to destroy* <u>John</u>, *but Jesus has come that* <u>John</u> *might have eternal life.*

WEDNESDAY: Write it. Write the verse and then what it says about:

✦ *Others:* Respond, serve, and love as Jesus would.

✦ *Me:* Specific attitudes, choices, or habits.

✦ *God:* His love, mercy, holiness, peace, joy, etc.

PRIVATE WORLD JOURNAL

I am grateful for—I praise You for—I am feeling—I am thinking—I need help with

PRIVATE WORLD DEVOTIONS *(Continued)*

THURSDAY: Memorize it. Take the verse with you—write it on a card or put it in your phone, iPod, or PDA. Go over it throughout the day so that it begins to *live* in your heart and mind.

FRIDAY: Pray it. Personalize the verse as you pray for yourself or for others or in praise to God. To pray is literally "to think about." Try thinking out loud or writing in your **PRIVATE WORLD JOURNAL.**

SATURDAY: Share it. Ask the Lord to bring someone to mind or in your path today who needs good news. Don't be shy—just let it out! Whether you IM, write, text, tell, or send it, the joy of God's Word will flow from your heart into theirs.

PRAYER REQUESTS

Date	Name	Need	Answer

PRIVATE WORLD JOURNAL

*I am grateful for—I praise You for—I am
feeling—I am thinking—I need help with*

NOTES

CHAPTER 3

MIRACLE WITHIN

KEY SCRIPTURE

I am a debtor both to Greeks and to barbarians, both to wise and to unwise. So, as much as is in me, I am ready to preach the gospel to you who are in Rome also. For I am not ashamed of the gospel of Christ, for it is the power of God to salvation for everyone who believes, for the Jew first and also for the Greek.

—Romans 1:14–16

THIS REALLY HAPPENED!

The day started out sunny with great promise of a fun day on Lake Burton. Family and friends were gathered for a relaxing weekend, and Ashley Thomas couldn't wait to head out on the Jet Ski across the lake.

She had been riding for a while when a storm suddenly came up, and the rain began to fall in what looked and felt like broken glass. It was definitely time to head in, but she was worried about a family friend who was less experienced. She stopped in the lake to wait for him, but with the sheets of rain coming down, he didn't see her until it was too late.

Ashley was hit full speed, head-on. Thrown from her Jet Ski, her injuries were massive; her body was torn open by the impact. For several hours, Ashley hovered between life and death as her family and friends prayed that God would spare her life. Doctors gave little hope.

If you meet Ashley today, she will more than likely tell you the story as she pulls up her shirt a bit to show you the scar on her midriff. She is proud of it. "Here is where God put His finger and healed me," she proudly says.

WHY KNOW IT?

✦ Only one-third of American teenagers (34%) are born-again Christians.[1]

✦ 43% of American teenagers talk to family or friends about religious matters in a typical day.[2]

transfuse (trans FYOOZ); to cause to pass from one to another; transmit

This first step to personal and campus evangelism is yours. It is not an "I'm better than you" attitude. It is, "Let me show you where God put His finger and made me whole."

Although most of the people sitting around you in church are here today because they have met Christ, you must never forget that our churches, schools, and communities are full of those whose wounds are still fresh.

Paul, a bondservant of Jesus Christ, called to be an apostle, separated to the gospel of God which He promised before through His prophets in the Holy Scriptures, concerning His Son Jesus Christ our Lord, who was born of the seed of David according to the flesh, and declared to be the Son of God with power

*according to the Spirit of holiness, by the
resurrection from the dead. . . . To all who are
in Rome, beloved of God, called to be saints:
Grace to you and peace from God our Father
and the Lord Jesus Christ.* **—Romans 1:1–4, 7**

One of the most dynamic and revolutionary leaders of the Christian faith was the apostle Paul. In his letter to the Romans, Paul has one objective and that is to *transform* rather than *inform*.

In the book of Romans, the apostle Paul lays out the major themes of salvation:

✦ *Redemption*. Christ's death exchanged for our sin. He paid the price to "buy us back" so that we could have eternal life.

✦ *Justification*. Through Christ's atoning death on the cross, we are made "just as if" we had never sinned.

✦ *Grace*. Salvation is a gift; it is God's Riches at Christ's Expense.

For the next few weeks, we will study what motivated Paul to risk his life and give his all so that others might know Christ.

As you see how God used Paul to ignite a revolution, you will also be motivated to start a revolution that radically changes your family, school, community, church, country—and, yes, maybe even the world!

infuse (in FYOOZ) : to cause to be permeated with something (as a principle or quality) that alters usually for the better

*I am a debtor both to Greeks and to barbarians,
both to wise and to unwise. So, as much as is
in me, I am ready to preach the gospel to you
who are in Rome also. For I am not ashamed of*

the gospel of Christ, for it is the power of God to salvation for everyone who believes, for the Jew first and also for the Greek. —**Romans 1:14–16**

Paul's plan to preach the gospel to the Romans was based on three things:

1. A burden for others (v. 14).

2. A bold confidence (v. 15).

3. A belief that all people need Christ (v. 16).

So, as much as is in me—Something deep inside gave Paul his boldness, something that was burning within. Literally, in the Greek language, Paul is saying, "I am willing (my part) to do God's will (God's part)."

Can you claim these three motivations? Write your name in each line:

_____ has a burden for others.

_____ has bold confidence to share the gospel.

_____ believes that all men need Christ.

   This burning passion to share the gospel has been described by some as a "holy heartburn." Remember when Jesus appeared to the disciples on the road to Emmaus after His resurrection? "They said to one another, 'Did not our heart burn within us while He talked with us on the road, and while He opened the Scriptures to us?'" (Luke 24:32). True salvation occurs first in our hearts and then is carried out in our actions.

Paul was never too shy to talk about the miracle that transformed him on the road to Damascus. What are some of the thoughts that go through your mind when you think about sharing Christ one on one with people? Choose one statement that is currently true of you:

+ Fear of being criticized.

+ Don't know what to say.

+ Not sure I have anything to share.

+ Boldness and excitement about the opportunity!

Which one would you *like* to choose?

History has been traditionally divided as BC (before Christ) or AD (*Anno Domini* in Latin, or, "in the year of our Lord"). But don't be surprised if you see the new terms BCE (before common era) or CE (common era). This designation is a direct attempt to remove the significance of the life of Jesus Christ.

Few people have consistently used their testimony as much as the apostle Paul. He not only broke his story down into simple, powerful pieces, he also used his personal story in many different ways depending on the need. Paul never missed an opportunity to talk about how Jesus changed his life, whether it was to the Hebrews or to the Greeks—two very different people groups in his day. He wanted everyone to know that God transformed his life from the inside out and that He could do the same for them!

Think about the people you know at school who do not know Christ. You may stay away from them because of the choices they make, but is there a way you could show them friendship without being involved in their lifestyle? How did Jesus do it?

GROUP DISCUSSION

Discuss at least three ways to reach out in friendship to people who do not know Christ.

---

diffuse (di FYOOZ)**:** to pour out and permit or cause to spread freely; to extend, scatter

Paul had a definite "BC" and "AD" life, meaning that his life completely and radically changed after he encountered Christ. His call to salvation was as personal as you could get. One day he was persecuting and killing Christians, and the next he was transformed by the power of the living Christ. Jesus came looking for him personally. Paul's life required a drastic and divine intervention.

Paul Shares His Testimony

Paul was brought before many crowds from the town center to the magistrates and governors of the land. Each time, without fail, he passionately told his story and was careful to highlight whatever was necessary to interact with the listeners.

Here is Paul's testimony, as recorded in the book of Acts:

1. I have not always lived for Christ.

I am indeed a Jew, born in Tarsus of Cilicia, but brought up in this city at the feet of Gamaliel, taught according to the strictness of our fathers' law, and was zealous toward God as you all are today. I persecuted this Way to the death, binding and delivering into prisons both men and women. —**Acts 22:3–4**

Paul was not merely an unbeliever; he hated and even tortured and killed Christians! That's "not living for Christ" at its most extreme.

2. I realized my need because God showed it to me.

Then he fell to the ground, and heard a voice saying to him, "Saul, Saul, why are you persecuting Me?" And he said, "Who are You, Lord?" Then the Lord said, "I am Jesus, whom you are persecuting. It is hard for you to kick against the goads." —**Acts 9:4–5**

In Bible times, the ox was a frequently used beast of burden. Instead of obeying the driver and submitting to his leading, the stubborn oxen usually first tried kicking against the sharpened sticks. Paul had probably often seen this occur as he walked through the cities and byways.

The Lord used it here to describe Paul's heart, which had kicked in vain at the salvation of Christ. He spent months resisting the pull of God on his life. But the moment his struggling ended, a revolution took place within him greater than anything he had ever known.

3. I made a personal commitment by faith to Christ.

*So I said, "What shall I do, Lord?" And the
Lord said to me, "Arise and go into Damascus,
and there you will be told all things which
are appointed for you to do."* —**Acts 22:10**

Once a hater of all things Christian, Paul found himself in surrender to the hands of the One who had been
his enemy. The surrender was complete. Peace was his
at last.

4. Christ has done a miracle in my life.

*Then [Paul] said, "The God of our fathers
has chosen you that you should know
His will, and see the Just One, and hear
the voice of His mouth. For you will be
His witness to all men of what you have
seen and heard."* —**Acts 22:14–15**

Paul's personal encounter with Jesus was all over
in a few moments, but it lasted until his dying day. In
fact, through the pages of Scripture, his conversion still
speaks and will continue to do so throughout eternity.

One thing you will note as you read the three Acts
accounts of Paul sharing his testimony (Acts 9, 22,
26) is that Paul always used the present tense when telling his story. He never spoke only about "that day," but
about how "that day" affects "this day."

Paul's outline from two thousand years ago is still applicable to your testimony today. You can use this same
outline to write your testimony.

Write Your Personal Testimony

Think about your personal salvation story. Using the outline below, write one to three sentences about your personal story for each point.

1. I have not always lived for Christ.

(Note: If you came to faith in Christ as a young child, then you can give a recent testimony of a genuine, memorable time when you had a spiritual experience with the Lord. Perhaps He spoke to you about a specific sin or walked with you through fear, anxiety, doubt, or insecurity. The only requirement of an effective testimony is that it be genuine.)

2. I realized my need because God showed it to me.

How? Did someone talk with you? Did you hear a sermon, read a passage of Scripture, hear a verse? Describe it.

For every person with a dramatic "Damascus Road" conversion story, there are a thousand more people with "Timothy" stories—that is, people who have been taught the Scriptures ever since they were children (2 Timothy 3:15). God uses both!

3. I made a personal commitment by faith to Christ.

How did you do this? What did you pray?

_____

_____

_____

4. Christ has done a miracle in my life.

The Lord does miracles in our lives every day. In a culture committed to evil, you have walked strong and true to the Word of God. That is something to write and talk about.

How did Christ change you? How does He walk with you every day? How does your relationship with Him affect your decisions, choices, lifestyle, and relationships?

_____

_____

_____

Now that you have sentences, try putting them all together in one paragraph and editing down to an easy-to-share story. Ask your accountability partner and/or your parents to look at it and help you to learn it well enough to share it.

_____

_____

_____

When sharing your testimony, you must remember that it is not within your power to make a person listen or respond. Your responsibility is to share the good news, and you must have faith that God will do the rest.

You might be having trouble writing your entire personal testimony at once. If so, remember that *salvation* is the all-inclusive word that describes what God has done and is doing in your life.

What is ONE THING that you could share this week with someone about one part of your salvation story:

✦ The past—what He *did* in your life

_____

_____

✦ The present—what He *is doing* in your life

_____

_____

✦ The future—what He *will do* in your life

_____

_____

Paul said, "If anyone is in Christ, he is a new creation; old things have passed away; behold, all things have become new" (2 Corinthians 5:17). He spoke this from a personal point of view. He lived it.

This verse describes important truths about every person who has put his or her faith in Christ.

In Christ, you have:

✦ *A new position*. In Christ, you are a part of a new family. You are in the family God.

✦ *A new personality*. You don't have to be weak, afraid, or insecure. A new confidence lives within you.

✦ *A new potential*. You realize that, if you want to, you can break free from the past—from habits, temptation, and sin—and begin again.

You must have faith. You must *believe* (cling to, rely on, and trust in) God!

FUSE BOX

A changed heart is possible because:
Salvation is exclusive—that is, only God can do it.
Salvation is extensive—"all things are made new"
(2 Corinthians 5:17; emphasis added).
Salvation is the chance to live again by faith.

NOTES

Do all the good you can.
In all the ways you can.
In all the places you can.
At all the times you can.
By all the means you can.
To all the people you can.
As long as ever you can.
—Attributed to John Wesley

PRIVATE WORLD DEVOTIONS

MONDAY: See it. Read the surrounding passages or chapter for the Key Scripture so that you can get an understanding of the background and context. This helps you to really *see* the verse.

TUESDAY: Hear it. Read the daily Key Scripture and/or surrounding passage out loud, putting your name in, if applicable. For example, <u>John</u> *can do all things through Christ. Thieves have come to destroy* <u>John</u>, *but Jesus has come that* <u>John</u> *might have eternal life.*

WEDNESDAY: Write it. Write the verse and then what it says about:

✦ *Others:* Respond, serve, and love as Jesus would.

✦ *Me:* Specific attitudes, choices, or habits.

✦ *God:* His love, mercy, holiness, peace, joy, etc.

PRIVATE WORLD JOURNAL

I am grateful for—I praise You for—I am feeling—I am thinking—I need help with

PRIVATE WORLD DEVOTIONS *(Continued)*

THURSDAY: Memorize it. Take the verse with you—write it on a card or put it in your phone, iPod, or PDA. Go over it throughout the day so that it begins to *live* in your heart and mind.

FRIDAY: Pray it. Personalize the verse as you pray for yourself or for others or in praise to God. To pray is literally "to think about." Try thinking out loud or writing in your **PRIVATE WORLD JOURNAL.**

SATURDAY: Share it. Ask the Lord to bring someone to mind or in your path today who needs good news. Don't be shy—just let it out! Whether you IM, write, text, tell, or send it, the joy of God's Word will flow from your heart into theirs.

PRAYER REQUESTS

Date	Name	Need	Answer

PRIVATE WORLD JOURNAL

I am grateful for—I praise You for—I am feeling—I am thinking—I need help with

NOTES

CHAPTER 4

MOTIVATED BY THE MULTITUDES

KEY SCRIPTURE

The harvest truly is great, but the laborers are few. Therefore pray the Lord of the harvest to send out laborers into His harvest.

— Luke 10:2

THIS REALLY HAPPENED!

Katie loved going to the skateboard park week after week. She was one of the few girls there who competed in tournaments; most of them just hung out to watch the guys. She got to be friends with a few of the guys who were skateboarders, but she was troubled by their lifestyle. They didn't know the Lord, and their language and hobbies were pretty bad. Katie prayed, "Lord, how can I, just one Christian girl, make a difference and win these guys to Christ?"

Katie thought, *Well, one thing I'm good at, other than skateboarding, is baking cookies!* So she started bringing homemade chocolate-chip cookies to the skate park each week. The only thing the guys had to do to get the cookies was to take a Christian tract that explained the gospel. That was a no-brainer, because most of them threw the tracts away as soon as she wasn't looking.

But one guy did read it, and he watched Katie. She was happy every week even though she didn't party. He decided he needed to know more, so he approached her in private. Katie took the tract and led Ken to Christ one Saturday. He, in turn, brought two other guys, and Katie gave out two more tracts.

All three of the guys came to Student Leadership University in Orlando the next year with Katie as she continued to show them the love of God and how to grow in Christ.

Baking cookies is a small thing that leads to big changes—and to transformed lives!

WHY KNOW IT?

✦ 55% of born-again Christians claim they have shared their faith with a non-Christian.[1]

✦ 49% of born-again Christians shared their faith in Christ in the past year taking a non-Christian friend to church so they could hear the gospel. [2]

✦ 21% of born-again Christians shared their faith in Christ with a non-Christian person in the past year by sending letters or e-mails explaining aspects of their faith and encouraging them to consider it more closely.[3]

transfuse (trans FYOOZ) ; to cause to pass from one to another; transmit

Students all across your school and community are lost without Christ. They are roaming from one relationship to another, one party to another, looking for real life. Christ in His love wants to reach them, but He needs you.

You may ask, "Are you worried, Lord, that they won't find the truth about salvation?" "No," He says, "because I'm counting on you to reach them."

I am a debtor both to Greeks and to barbarians,
both to wise and to unwise. —**Romans 1:14**

Paul felt he was a debtor to Christ for all He had done for him. He felt obligated to tell others of the good news that he had been given. How would he pay that debt? It would take preaching to all men—"Greeks and barbarians, wise and unwise."

In other words, Paul preached the gospel to:

✦ Those who were religious—and those who weren't.

✦ Those who wanted to hear—and those who didn't.

infuse (in FYOOZ) : to cause to be permeated with something (as a principle or quality) that alters usually for the better

In the first century AD, the entire known world revolved around the Mediterranean. All the great civilizations grew up near this sea, which was considered to be the center of the earth. (*Mediterranean* literally means "the land at the middle of the earth.") Three nations of that time were strong enough and great enough to leave their marks on other nations forever: Rome, Greece, and Israel.[4]

Paul traveled and preached across the Mediterranean nations as the Holy Spirit directed him. No one has ever preached to more diverse groups than he did. We read throughout the book of Acts that Paul presented the gospel to:

✦ government officials;

✦ prisoners;

+ townspeople;

+ idol worshipers;

+ Jewish synagogues;

+ Athenian philosophers.

Paul was a brilliant man and a great writer. So all of this preaching must have been easy for him, right? Or was it?

By his own admission, Paul's presentation skills and appearance weren't much. He admits, "I am untrained in speech" (2 Corinthians 11:6). And he is aware of what his critics say about him: "His bodily presence is weak, and his speech is contemptible" (2 Corinthians 10:10).

Ouch! Not very flattering stuff. Why would God pick such a man to bring the gospel to the known world?

+ *Because of his intense love for the Lord Jesus.*
  Paul said, "For to me, to live is Christ and to die is gain" (Philippians 1:21).

+ *Because he saw people as Jesus saw them.* He saw each person as in need of a Savior, regardless of race, creed, or background.

+ *Because of what he had been through.* Because of his education and social training, he was uniquely suited to relate to the Jews, the Romans, and the Greeks.

Understand that every moment of your life contributes to your ability to represent Christ, both the good and the bad. Give it all you've got every day, because Christ deserves your best.

This great apostle preached with the same passion to a runaway slave as he did to a Roman jailor, and to a businesswoman by the river as he did to a governor or king. He saw the multitudes through the eyes of compassion.

This is the secret to a life of caring about others—that is, to see people in the same way that Jesus saw them.

Then Jesus went about all the cities and villages, teaching in their synagogues, preaching the gospel of the kingdom, and healing every sickness and every disease among the people. But when He saw the multitudes, He was moved with compassion for them, because they were weary and scattered, like sheep having no shepherd. Then He said to His disciples, "The harvest truly is plentiful, but the laborers are few. Therefore pray the Lord of the harvest to send out laborers into His harvest."
—Matthew 9:36–38

In this passage, the robe of glory is pulled back, and we see the tender heart of Jesus:

When He saw the multitudes. Jesus has the unique ability to see what the casual observer does not see. He sees their outward actions, but He sees deep into the heart. You might say He wears spiritual bifocals!

Because they were weary. He could see the people's immediate needs—they were tired to the point of exhaustion. They had come to the end of both their physical and emotional abilities; they could not take another step. In other words, they wanted to give up on life.

> If we can but show the whole world that being committed to Christ is no tame, humdrum, sheltered monotony but the most thrilling, exciting adventure the human spirit can ever know, then those who have been standing outside the church and looking askance at Christ would come crowding in to pay allegiance to Him. And we might well expect the greatest revival since Pentecost!
> —Dr. James Stewart

Scattered, like sheep. He could see their ultimate need—they were lost and needed a Savior. He saw them as a flock of sheep scattered across the mountain ridges after being chased by wolves. In that flock would be baby sheep, frightened and alone, separated and orphaned from their parents. Other sheep might be bleeding from the cactus and sharp rocks, and still others would be suffering from broken limbs from where they fell off of a ridge and came near to death.

Having no shepherd. These sheep were without protection and without anyone to care for them.

Jesus saw people's suffering, pain, and needs, and "He was moved with compassion for them." The Greek word translated "compassion" in this verse is from the word *agonize*, or *to suffer.*

Our Savior suffers with us as we should with others. "For we do not have a High Priest who cannot sympathize with our weaknesses, but was in all points tempted as we are, yet without sin" (Hebrews 4:15).

diffuse (di FYOOZ): to pour out and permit or cause to spread freely; to extend, scatter

At a recent student evangelism conference, the hotel elevators were slow because of the huge crowd. When the doors opened, people squeezed in so they wouldn't be stranded. At one particular floor, the door opened, and three students who were obviously not with the Christian conference got on. Covered with tattoos and piercings, they had a hollow, empty look. The church crowd slid to the back of the elevator and didn't say a word.

The doors opened again, and the students stepped off without exchanging a word.

After the guys left, the Christian students said to one another, "Hey, I guess we should have invited them to our concert." "Yeah, we should have." "Oh well. They were just weird anyway." And with that they walked away.

No one saw the teens through the eyes of Christ. Instead of being moved to share the good news, the "church kids" moved away to their own comfort zone.

ASK YOURSELF

Have you ever been a part of a scene like that at your school? What did you do? What should you do?

What is ONE THING you could do to demonstrate the genuine, unconditional love of Christ to someone this week?

> We see problems in people. Jesus sees potential.

Every year, Student Leadership University takes students to the Louvre Museum in Paris. There they visit the *Venus de Milo*, one of the most famous pieces of ancient Greek sculpture. It is believed to depict Aphrodite (called Venus by the Romans), the Greek goddess of love and beauty. This sculpture has been duly praised by artists and critics, who regard it as the epitome of graceful female beauty, despite the fact that her arms have been lost.

Venus is a depiction of many Christian students. She is nice to look at, but cold-hearted, with lips that do not speak and no arms to reach out to others with.

We know the price of everything we want to buy—iPods, CDs, movies, clothes, jewelry, concert tickets, electronic games, cell phones—but we don't value people or see the value in their lives.

Jesus values every life as a friend worth dying for. "Greater love has no one than this, than to lay down one's life for his friends" (John 15:13).

Are you clear in your own mind of the great value you have to Jesus?

_____

_____

_____

You must understand Christ's deep love for you before you can tell others how much God loves them. Choose at least one person in each of your classes who you will commit to pray for:

1. _____ 2. _____

3. _____ 4. _____

5. _____ 6. _____

For every problem, Jesus has a solution. In the case of lost sheep, He is the true Shepherd, but He uses you to bring in the sheep.

He says, "The harvest truly is great, but the laborers are few. Therefore pray the Lord of the harvest to send out laborers into His harvest" (Luke 10:2). In other words, many people are searching for eternal life, but few Christians are willing to give of themselves to reach them. Jesus used the illustration of a farmer, one who rolls up his sleeves and gets his hands dirty, while working in the field to harvest the ripe crops.

If you are a follower of Christ, it will cost you time, tears, and money to share the gospel with others. You are working with Christ in this effort to bring in the lost. He never asks you to do what He hasn't already done.

[FUSE BOX]

Success in witnessing is simply sharing the good news of Jesus in the power of the Holy Spirit and leaving the results to God.

PRIVATE WORLD DEVOTIONS

MONDAY: See it. Read the surrounding passages or chapter for the Key Scripture so that you can get an understanding of the background and context. This helps you to really *see* the verse.

TUESDAY: Hear it. Read the daily Key Scripture and/or surrounding passage out loud, putting your name in, if applicable. For example, John *can do all things through Christ. Thieves have come to destroy* John, *but Jesus has come that* John *might have eternal life.*

WEDNESDAY: Write it. Write the verse and then what it says about:

+ *Others:* Respond, serve, and love as Jesus would.
+ *Me:* Specific attitudes, choices, or habits.
+ *God:* His love, mercy, holiness, peace, joy, etc.

PRIVATE WORLD JOURNAL

I am grateful for—I praise You for—I am feeling—I am thinking—I need help with

PRIVATE WORLD DEVOTIONS *(Continued)*

THURSDAY: Memorize it. Take the verse with you—write it on a card or put it in your phone, iPod, or PDA. Go over it throughout the day so that it begins to *live* in your heart and mind.

FRIDAY: Pray it. Personalize the verse as you pray for yourself or for others or in praise to God. To pray is literally "to think about." Try thinking out loud or writing in your **PRIVATE WORLD JOURNAL.**

SATURDAY: Share it. Ask the Lord to bring someone to mind or in your path today who needs good news. Don't be shy—just let it out! Whether you IM, write, text, tell, or send it, the joy of God's Word will flow from your heart into theirs.

PRAYER REQUESTS

Date	Name	Need	Answer

PRIVATE WORLD JOURNAL

I am grateful for—I praise You for—I am feeling—I am thinking—I need help with

NOTES

CHAPTER 5

PRAYING FOR THE LOST

KEY SCRIPTURE

Do you not know that to whom you present yourselves slaves to obey, you are that one's slaves whom you obey, whether of sin leading to death, or of obedience leading to righteousness?
— **Romans 6:16**

THIS REALLY HAPPENED!

Diane remembers the night her friends were laughing at the "Jesus freaks." She joined in and said, "Yeah, the last thing I ever want to be is one of those." They spent the next hour talking about the students who were handing out pamphlets about Jesus and inviting them to Bible studies. Yet in the back of her mind, Diane remembered Mark, who kept talking to her about Jesus.

He would show up at parties but just sit in the chair and smile. He wouldn't drink, smoke, or party with girls, and no one could really figure him out. He kept giving Diane pamphlets, and one night she told him, "I know all about religion. I've been to church my whole life."

Mark tried to explain, "It's not about religion. It's about knowing Jesus personally."

"Forget it," she told him, "and leave me alone."

Mark left the room quietly with his head down, and Diane was sorry that she had hurt him. What she didn't know was that he committed to pray for her every day until she would come to know a personal faith in Christ.

A few weeks later, Diane stood in a crowd of ten thousand people at a rock concert and listened as the lead singer blasphemed God. No one else seemed to notice as the crowd screamed and rocked on, but she did. In the midst of the noise, all she could hear was God speaking to her heart: "Make a decision. Who will you live for?"

She remembered some of the things Mark had told her and prayed, "Lord, I give You my life. Come into my heart."

Diane will tell you that her life changed drastically that night, and she called Mark the next morning. "What happened to me? Can you come and explain?"

That day, Mark told her that God had answered his prayers for her life, and he opened the Scriptures to show her God's love.

WHY KNOW IT?

✦ There are approximately 180,000 new cult recruits every year.[1]

✦ There are 19 major world religions, which are subdivided into a total of 270 large religious groups, and many smaller ones. More than 34,000 separate Christian groups have been identified in the world.[2]

transfuse (trans FYOOZ) : to cause to pass from one to another; transmit

Do you think that sometimes we give up, give in, and just plain quit too soon? Have you shared the gospel with friends who walked away or put you down, and you just stopped believing that they would ever listen?

We must remember that our compassion for others and our faith in God's willingness to answer our prayers are not to be contingent on their response. Never take it personally. They are rejecting Christ, not you.

Would it help if you knew that Jesus Himself prays for you and for them? We are to keep believing, to keep sharing, to keep praying.

I do not pray for these alone, but also for those who will believe in Me through their word; that they all may be one, as You, Father, are in Me, and I in You; that they also may be one in Us, that the world may believe that You sent Me. And the glory which You gave Me I have given them, that they may be one just as We are one: I in them, and You in Me; that they may be made perfect in one, and that the world may know that You have sent Me, and have loved them as You have loved Me. —**John 17:18–23**

Jesus prayed for His disciples in John 17. This chapter is sometimes called "The Lord's Prayer," because it is a personal, public prayer that Jesus prayed for us while on the earth.

infuse (in FYOOZ)̈ : to cause to be permeated with something (as a principle or quality) that alters usually for the better

In John 17, Jesus has been praying for eighteen verses for His disciples. Next, He adds *you* to His prayer and those you will lead to Christ! "I do not pray for these alone [His disciples on earth at the time], but also for those who will believe in Me through their word" (v. 20). That includes you!

 Jesus prayed that you will be triumphant in your mission to share the message of the love of Christ.

Wow! If Jesus Himself prays for you, how can you help but be successful?

When He prayed for you, Jesus's first words were that you would be unified with other Christians for a specific purpose. He prayed "that they all may be one, as You, Father, are in Me, and I in You; that they also may be one in Us, that the world may believe that You sent Me" (v. 21).

Your specific goal: "that the world may believe that You sent Me." What an honor! You get to show the world that *Jesus Christ is the One sent from God.* It's an incredible honor and opportunity, but how do we do it?

If Jesus prays for you to do it, then He must also have a plan on *how* to do it. He says it starts with unity with other Christians.

◆ Accountability partners who help you stay faithful.

◆ Christian friends who can encourage and pray for you.

◆ A group of believers called the church.

Before a movie is released, a trailer is shown. A trailer is a compilation of small bits of the movie. The movie promoters know that people will watch the trailer for phrases or expressions that they can relate to or that they like, will watch how the actors react and interact, and decide from that whether or not they will give the movie a chance.

The church is often like that movie trailer. We are *sent out* to talk about the Word of God and the gift of salvation through Christ's death on the cross and to give people a small preview of the amazing glory and grace of God. How we present that message and the value we give to it by our actions will cause many to decide whether or not it is worth looking into. People are watching our lives to see if we have anything real to believe in, and they are watching to see if we are part of a group they could belong to.

There are many, many Christians at your school of varying church denominations. Have you considered establishing a place where many of you could come together, pray together, encourage one another, and establish a testimony to the rest of your school?

THINK ABOUT IT

It is so important that you belong to a group of believers that are unified in their message, a message of love, that Christ chose to make it a major point in His prayer.

Your youth group at church is not just a social club. It is divinely chosen by God to be a place where lost students will find the Shepherd. They will find Him because they see Him pouring out of you and your friends.

Students are famous for cliques. You can be included or excluded on a number of technicalities. Girls and guys change their hair, add a piercing, get a tattoo, dress differently, try drugs, experiment with sex—all of this for a chance to belong to a group, for a

Dr. Bill Bright, founder of Campus Crusade, was devoted to being a Christlike man. He focused his entire life on evangelism. And thousands of ministries around the world have been touched by his influence.

Dr. Bright was once asked how he was able to work with so many different denominations and such a variety of doctrines and cultures. He gave a simple answer: "I just focus on Jesus. We can all agree to work for the furtherance of the pure gospel that Christ died, rose from the dead, and offers the gift of eternal life to everyone."

Today, Dr. Bright's *Jesus* film has now been translated into 910 languages, viewed by 5.4 billion people worldwide, and it has been the means by which over 200 million people have professed faith in Christ.

If Dr. Bright were alive today, he would say, "Keep the main thing— Jesus—as the main thing." How long are you willing to wait for God's vision?

chance to be *liked!* Being accepted into a group is a very powerful need for students.

The Christian who is "on call" for Christ recognizes this need and intensely works toward broadening the church group of believers to welcome everyone, to love everyone in a way that only Christ can love. That is, not as the world loves—what you look like, smell like, how cool you might be. But as Jesus loves, blind to all but the value of soul created by God.

Christ is counting on you to *let them know* who He is and how much He loves them. He specifically prays here for the unbeliever to become a believer; that they might *know* Him. What can you do this week to show the love of Christ to someone who doesn't yet know Him?

What is ONE THING you can do to bring about a change in your youth group so that it becomes a place where the love of God is the center of it?

diffuse (di FYOOZ) : to pour out and permit or cause to spread freely; to extend, scatter

How can you banish cliques in your youth group? List some ideas below:

_____

_____

_____

◆ Imagine that you are the new kid on the block this week at church. How would it feel to walk in to your youth group?

_____

_____

_____

◆ What can you do to establish a welcome team?

_____

_____

_____

◆ Can you call, e-mail, write to visitors during the week?

_____

_____

_____

✦ How will you bring new people into the youth group?

As you make arrangements for a Bible club on campus, prepare to share your faith, and commit to live a public life of purity, there is one thing that must precede all of this, and that is prayer.

✦ Set a regular time for prayer. What day/ time works with your schedule? Write two possibilities:

✦ *Set a place for prayer.* Circle two choices to look into:

School   your house   church   friend's house

✦ *Bring others in to pray with you.* Start a list of friends who you can invite to join you in your prayer vigil for the lost:

Choose those who will be faithful. It is better to start with a few who are sincere than with many just to have a crowd. It's not hard when you do it the way Christ did it: You start with one who invites another, who brings a brother/sister, who brings a friend, who tells another, and so on. It is exciting to be in on a direct order from Christ and to watch Him use you to begin it!

If we are to make a difference in the lives of those without Christ, we must pray specifically and confidently. Jesus did it. Jesus did it for you.

In the back of this study guide is your "I Believe in Prayer" Journal. Here you should record:

- ✦ Names of those you are praying for.

- ✦ Personal needs they have such as salvation, physical healing, family communication, spiritual strength, etc.

What do you want to be written about you in your yearbook? Do you want to be remembered as one who cared more about others than about your own popularity? As a person who prayed for others with consistency?

Write what you would like to see said about you:

Never share others' personal needs publicly. Many people have been victims of gossip that began in a prayer group. What was voiced as concern became damaging gossip as the word traveled as a "prayer request." Take care to be faithful in keeping a person's trust. You can pray for their need and request specific prayers, but never share private information.

If you do, chances are that you forfeit the opportunity to influence that person for Christ and damage your own testimony of being a caring, compassionate person. That would be a sad thing.

Specific Prayers for Others:

✦ For protection against the enemy, Satan.

> *Simon, Simon! Indeed, Satan has asked for you, that he may sift you as wheat. But I have prayed for you, that your faith should not fail; and when you have returned to Me, strengthen your brethren.* **—Luke 22:31–32**

Jesus's prayer for Peter demonstrates the urgency and importance of praying for other believers to be protected from Satan's temptations and attacks.

✦ That the Lord would send another witness.

In Acts 7, Stephen preached a powerful message of Christ's redemption just before he was martyred for his faith. Those in the crowd turned and laid their garments at the feet of a man named Saul, who would later become the great apostle Paul.

Saul did not come to Christ for some time after that, but we can be sure that the witness of Stephen made a lasting impression on his life and on his ministry. Likewise, it may not be your verbal witness that God uses but someone else's. Pray that others will be sent who can reach your lost friend through their testimony.

✦ That the habit or pride holding them back would be broken.

> *Do you not know that to whom you present yourselves slaves to obey, you are that one's slaves whom you obey, whether of sin leading to death, or of obedience leading to righteousness?* **—Romans 6:16**

Those who do not know the freedom of God's grace also do not understand that certain habits and attitudes are keeping them from surrendering to God's will and to salvation. Pray that these strongholds of their hearts would be broken.

✦ **That they might know there is only one Savior.**

> *This is eternal life, that they may know You, the only true God, and Jesus Christ whom You have sent.* —**John 17:3**

How will a person ever know that Jesus is *the* Way when so many religious and cult groups are calling themselves the only way to God? Pray for the truth of God's Word to be evident, for the eternal life that is available when a person receives Christ as the only true Savior.

✦ **For conviction of sin.**

> *And when He [the Holy Spirit] has come, He will convict the world of sin, and of righteousness, and of judgment.*—**John 16:8**

Our responsibility is not to judge others' sin, but to pray that others will be convicted by God of their sin. Sin is not relative to a situation; it is not an opinion to be decided.

✦ **For repentance.**

> *I have not come to call the righteous, but sinners, to repentance.* —**Luke 5:32**

Conviction comes first, but it must be followed by repentance in order for salvation to be genuine. Only the Holy Spirit of God can convict a person of sin and lead him or her to repentance.

✦ **For surrender to the will of God.**

> *So he [Paul], trembling and astonished, said, "Lord, what do You want me to do?" Then the Lord said to him, "Arise and go into the city, and you will be told what you must do."* —**Acts 9:6**

Paul's conversion gives us a glimpse of genuine salvation. Saul, who once persecuted Christians, asks the Lord, "What do you want me to do?" This can only come about as we pray for a surrender to Christ.

✦ **For genuine faith.**

> But without faith it is impossible to please Him, for he who comes to God must believe that He is, and that He is a rewarder of those who diligently seek Him. —**Hebrews 11:6**

When you pray that others will understand God's Word, be sure to pray for God to give them faith to believe that understanding. Never forget that "without faith it is impossible to please Him." Faith is an integral part of salvation.

Confident Prayers:

✦ **Pray in faith.**

> And whatever things you ask in prayer, believing, you will receive. —**Matthew 21:22**

As we saw in Hebrews 11:6, faith pleases the Lord. He tells us to pray with faith, without any doubting (James 1:6). And if you have faith as small as a grain of mustard seed (which is very small!), then Jesus says that "nothing will be impossible for you" (Matthew 17:20). So pray in faith, with confidence that God will hear and answer you!

✦ **Pray in Christ's name.**

> If you ask anything in My name, I will do it. —**John 14:14**

We were all created with a free will. We cannot force a person to accept Christ. Christ will not force one to believe in Him. But we can pray for people, and we can share the gospel with them.

Your "I Believe in Prayer" Journal

Turn to your "I Believe in Prayer" Journal and write the name of one person who comes to your mind who needs Christ as Savior. Now select one of the scriptures above and take a few moments to pray for that person by inserting their name in the Scripture.

[FUSE BOX]

If you want to be a person of influence in sharing the gospel, you must begin by being known in your school and among your friends as a young man or woman who prays for others, who lives a consistently moral lifestyle, and who knows firsthand what he or she believes.

He who is greatest among you shall be your servant. That's a new definition of greatness. . . . It means that everybody can be great, because everybody can serve.

—Martin Luther King Jr.

PRIVATE WORLD DEVOTIONS

MONDAY: See it. Read the surrounding passages or chapter for the Key Scripture so that you can get an understanding of the background and context. This helps you to really *see* the verse.

TUESDAY: Hear it. Read the daily Key Scripture and/or surrounding passage out loud, putting your name in, if applicable. For example, <u>John</u> *can do all things through Christ. Thieves have come to destroy* <u>John</u>, *but Jesus has come that* <u>John</u> *might have eternal life.*

WEDNESDAY: Write it. Write the verse and then what it says about:

- ✦ *Others:* Respond, serve, and love as Jesus would.
- ✦ *Me:* Specific attitudes, choices, or habits.
- ✦ *God:* His love, mercy, holiness, peace, joy, etc.

PRIVATE WORLD JOURNAL

I am grateful for—I praise You for—I am feeling—I am thinking—I need help with

PRIVATE WORLD DEVOTIONS *(Continued)*

THURSDAY: Memorize it. Take the verse with you—write it on a card or put it in your phone, iPod, or PDA. Go over it throughout the day so that it begins to *live* in your heart and mind.

FRIDAY: Pray it. Personalize the verse as you pray for yourself or for others or in praise to God. To pray is literally "to think about." Try thinking out loud or writing in your **PRIVATE WORLD JOURNAL**.

SATURDAY: Share it. Ask the Lord to bring someone to mind or in your path today who needs good news. Don't be shy—just let it out! Whether you IM, write, text, tell, or send it, the joy of God's Word will flow from your heart into theirs.

PRAYER REQUESTS

Date	Name	Need	Answer

PRIVATE WORLD JOURNAL

*I am grateful for—I praise You for—I am
feeling—I am thinking—I need help with*

NOTES

CHAPTER 6

THE MOUNTAIN BEHIND US

KEY SCRIPTURE

Greater love has no one than this, than to lay down one's life for his friends.

— **John 15:13**

THIS REALLY HAPPENED!

Gloria grew up in a religious home. Every room displayed a cross with Jesus hanging on it. There was a big Bible in the living room, but no one ever opened it. Instead they went to church every Sunday and read from the bulletin. Gloria went to a private Christian school and was taught in all the traditions of her faith. She thought, *I know all the rules*.

When she became a teenager, her faith started to feel dead and boring. So she decided to bend the rules a bit and started experimenting with sex and alcohol. She felt guilty but thought, *There are a lot of students a lot worse than me. God would never keep me out of heaven*.

Soon she went further and further into sin, but it was always easy to find someone who was a "bigger sinner" than her, so she justified her behavior as "not that bad." The cross still hung on her wall. She still went to church. Surely that was enough.

One Sunday, she went to another church with a friend. This one was different. They actually smiled, the pastor told a joke, and the people seemed to enjoy being there. Gloria thought, *This is weird*. But she went back the next week.

This time she brought her Bible with her, and she listened to the sermon about the cross. She had heard this sermon many times—

about how Jesus died for her. But this time, the pastor didn't stop there. He started talking about *why* Jesus died for her and how He rose from the dead. Gloria remembers feeling a strange warming come over her heart as she listened.

Suddenly, it all made sense. Jesus was no longer on the cross. He rose from the dead, and this gave her a new purpose to live for. It wasn't a dead set of rules that she needed to live by, it was a living, loving Savior she needed to live for.

WHY KNOW IT?

✦ Crucifixion was a common form of execution in sixth to fourth century BC.

✦ Of all the religious leaders of the world, only Jesus Christ has risen from the dead.

transfuse (trans FYOOZ): to cause to pass from one to another; transmit

Life makes every attempt to steal away our faith and our identity in Christ. There are dark places where there seems to be nothing to hold on to, but not for the student who holds onto the truth of God. Do not hold on to anything of which the cross and resurrection of Jesus Christ are not central.

The apostle Paul had a secret that enabled him to renew his passion for God and for hurting people. His entire life was lived to tell others about the cross of Christ.

Now, normally it isn't cool to read someone else's journal, but Paul sent his for all to see and for our benefit.

> *Are they ministers of Christ?—I speak as a*
> *fool—I am more: in labors more abundant,*
> *in stripes above measure, in prisons more*
> *frequently, in deaths often. From the Jews five*
> *times I received forty stripes minus one. Three*
> *times I was beaten with rods; once I was stoned;*
> *three times I was shipwrecked; a night and a*
> *day I have been in the deep; in journeys often,*
> *in perils of waters, in perils of robbers, in perils*
> *of my own countrymen, in perils of the Gentiles,*
> *in perils in the city, in perils in the wilderness,*
> *in perils in the sea, in perils among false*
> *brethren; in weariness and toil, in sleeplessness*
> *often, in hunger and thirst, in fastings often, in*
> *cold and nakedness—besides the other things,*
> *what comes upon me daily: my deep concern*
> *for all the churches.—***2 Corinthians 11:23–28**

Beatings, prison, near death experiences, stoned, shipwrecked, lost at sea, traveling through floods, surrounded by thieves, hated and hunted, hiding in the wilderness, exhausted, starved, cold, naked. How would one man endure so much pain? In the midst of all this suffering, Paul wrote the book of Philippians, which is often called "the book of joy." His ability to endure hard times came from the joy of serving Christ and reaching others with the gospel. Christ was his first love.

infuse (in FYOOZ) to cause to be permeated with something (as a principle or quality) that alters usually for the better

 Where does your joy come from? In a time of stress and difficulty, are you ready to complain and quit?

Need a new perspective on life? Try this ONE THING: Keep this list of Paul's persecutions and difficulties with you for one week and study it. Every time a difficulty, disappointment, or stress comes up in your own life, compare it to Paul's list. Watch how quickly your outlook changes!

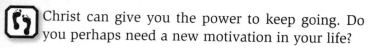

Christ can give you the power to keep going. Do you perhaps need a new motivation in your life?

By the way, what is your motivation for going to church each week?

_____

_____

_____

Paul continually preached the gospel of Christ by telling his story over and over to anyone who would listen and to many who wouldn't. He says that he was compelled by the death and resurrection of Christ to endure hardship and persecution.

The Passion of Jesus Christ

The last earthly days of Jesus's life are often referred to as the Passion. It began in the Garden of Gethsemane, a place where he went many times to pray. Knowing what was about to take place, He spent a last night there, agonizing in prayer.

He said to His disciples, "'My soul is swallowed up in sorrow—to the point of death. Remain here and stay awake with Me.' Going a little farther, He fell on His face, praying, 'My Father! If it is possible, let this cup pass from Me. Yet not as I will, but as You will'" (Matthew 26:38–39).

Jesus knew that He was about to face not just death, but agony. Note what He said: "My soul is swallowed up in sorrow" (v. 38). So much did Jesus dread the suffering that was about to come that He said to the Father, "If there is another way, let Me pass on this cup of suffering." But, of course, there wasn't another way. Let's see why . . .

Man Is Sinful
Adam sinned, and thus the fall from grace occurred. Every person who has ever been born, regardless of his or her talents or intellect, is a sinner. Romans 3:23 says, "For all have sinned and fall short of the glory of God."

God Is Holy
But God, who is infinitely holy, has no sin. He is, "Holy, holy, holy, Lord God Almighty, Who was and is and is to come!" (Revelation 4:8).

The Problem—Sin Separates Us from God
This contrast of God as holy and man as a sinner presents a huge problem—we are separated from God because of our sin. As long as we have sin in our lives, we cannot be in the presence of a holy God.

God does not categorize sin into "big sin" (like murder or child abuse) or "small sin" (like lying or cursing). Sin, *any* sin, separates man from God. God cannot allow sin into heaven, but He wants man with Him for all eternity.

The Solution—A Perfect Sacrifice for Sin
To solve the problem, He came Himself to earth to pay the price of man's sin, all of it. A sacrifice for the sin had to be made. In the Old Testament, God required that a spotless lamb be given as a sacrifice for the sin of the

people. But, He had promised a Savior since the beginning of time, and He sent Jesus.

Hebrews 9:22 tells us that "sins cannot be forgiven without blood to show death" (NCV). So God sent His only Son to shed His blood through death so He could forgive the sins of the world.

The "Cup" That Christ Drank

Jesus asked if the "cup" could pass from Him (Matthew 26:39). What do you suppose was in that cup? By taking the whole message of the New Testament, we have an idea of what He would have to drink in the cup.

◆ *Sin.* Jesus was the spotless Lamb of God. This Lamb took upon Himself the sins of the world and gave His perfect life in exchange. That's why His suffering was so intense.

◆ *Suffering.* Mel Gibson's movie *The Passion of the Christ* was controversial. If you've seen it, then those images are forever burned in your mind. The debate roared: did Gibson have to show so much gore and blood and pain? He did if he wanted to show the truth. There was much suffering in the cup Jesus drank because sin brings much suffering in the world.

◆ *Shame.* There was shame in the cup that Christ drank. He was beaten, spit on, and laughed at. He knew as He prayed that night in Gethsemane that He would have to endure this kind of shame and humiliation.

Why Did Christ Do It?

When Jesus was hanging on the cross, His persecutors taunted Him, "If You are the Son of God, come down from the cross" (Matthew 27:40). He could have come down, of course, but not if He wanted to fulfill the purpose for which He came to earth—to be the perfect sacrifice for our sins.

Jesus had the power to give His life and the power to take it back. Jesus knew He had to die to shed His blood for the forgiveness of our sins, so He faithfully endured the agony and shame of the cross.

That is love, a love we cannot define in earthly terms.

Think about how many crosses are worn every day at your school. You know that most of the people wearing them have no idea what this really means. Can you use a comment or compliment about their jewelry to give a personal testimony of what the cross means to you? Give it a try. Write three sentences here that you could say about your personal love for the cross of Christ:

John 15:13 says, "Greater love has no one than this, than to lay down one's life for his friends". It was the love of Christ that reached out to Saul as he persecuted and killed Christians and called him to a new life of proclaiming the gospel.

Paul never forgot that second chance, and he poured out his life to tell others about it.

1. _____

2. _____

3. _____

What Happened Next?

When Jesus's "cup" of sin, suffering, and shame was full, He cried out, "'Father, into Your hands I commit My spirit.' Having said this, He breathed His last" (Luke 23:46–47).

But was Jesus really dead? Or was this just a trick?

+ Was He just in a coma and then woke up from it later?

+ Did He just lie in a tomb for days without medical attention and then walk out?

+ Did He just pass out on the cross and then revive Himself later?

Let's look at what the Scripture has to say about Jesus's death and burial.

Jesus Was Legally Dead

> *When [the Roman soldiers] came to Jesus and saw that He was already dead, they did not break His legs. But one of the soldiers pierced His side with a spear, and immediately blood and water came out.* —**John 19:33–34**

Jesus was pronounced legally dead by the Roman soldiers who made their living knowing these things. When His side was pierced, "blood and water came out," which indicates that He was dead. Then He spent three days without medical attention in a sealed tomb.

Jesus's Body Was Guarded

> *On the next day . . . the chief priests and Pharisees gathered together to Pilate, saying, "Sir, we remember, while He was still alive, how that deceiver said, '**After three days I will rise.**' Therefore command that the tomb be made secure until the third day, lest His disciples come by night and steal Him away, and say to the people, 'He has risen from the dead.' So the last deception will be worse than the first." Pilate said to them, "You have a guard; go your way, make it as secure as you know how." So they went and made the tomb secure, sealing the stone and setting the guard.* —**Matthew 27:62–66**

Jesus's body was guarded by a special guard of Roman soldiers, the equivalent of our Special Forces. If a prisoner escaped under the watch of a Roman soldier, that soldier would have been forced to take that prisoner's penalty. In other words, if the prisoner was to die, then the soldier would die. If the prisoner was to be beaten, then the soldier would be beaten.

Had Jesus's body been stolen, the soldiers would have been put to death. You can be sure that they set a secure watch so that this could not happen.

Jesus Rose from the Dead!

> Now on the first day of the week, very early in the morning, they, and certain other women with them, came to the tomb bringing the spices which they had prepared. But they found the stone rolled away from the tomb. Then they went in and did not find the body of the Lord Jesus. . . . And it happened, as they were greatly perplexed about this, that behold, two men stood by them in shining garments. Then, as they were afraid and bowed their faces to the earth, they said to them, "Why do you seek the living among the dead? He is not here, but is risen!" —**Luke 24:1–6**

Jesus walked out through His own supernatural power. He rose from the dead. An angel rolled away the stone that sealed the tomb so that those who came to see could look inside. Amazing story! Spectacular? Unbelievable? No, just divine.

In the New Testament, the death of Christ is always, and necessarily, associated with His resurrection. Death without resurrection speaks only of hopeless defeat. A dead Savior is a contradiction in terms. Only a risen, victorious Savior has the power to communicate His redemption to those on whose behalf He has acted.

He is risen! He is risen indeed!

These are the words that give you hope every day for every breath and every thought and every need of your life.

---

diffuse (di FYOOZ): to pour out and permit or cause to spread freely; to extend, scatter

---

The Gospel of Jesus Christ

In 1 Corinthians 15:3–4, the apostle Paul gives us the whole gospel of Christ in two short verses: "I delivered to you first of all that which I also received: that Christ died for our sins according to the Scriptures, and that He was buried, and that He rose again the third day according to the Scriptures".

+ *That Christ died for our sins.* The central theme of the Bible is the cross: "Christ died for our sins." Without the cross, there is no salvation and there is no hope.

+ *According to the Scriptures.* The birth and death of the Savior, the Messiah, had been foretold throughout the Scriptures. As soon as man sinned, God promised a Savior. As a Jew, Saul knew all of these promises, but he refused to believe that they referred to Jesus. As a Christian, Paul knew them to be true. This was the Messiah, the Sent One.

+ *That He was buried.* If you are to effectively share the gospel of Christ, you must understand why the burial of Christ was so significant. If He was not buried and pronounced legally dead, then it is possible for Satan's liars to distort the truth of the resurrection. But, of course, we have seen that Jesus didn't just pass out or go into a coma; He actually died, and He was buried in a tomb guarded by Roman soldiers for three days.

◆ *And that He rose again the third day according to the Scriptures*. If we understand that Christ had to die on the cross as a substitution for our sin, then we can more fully comprehend that He had to rise from the dead. Jesus's resurrection demonstrated His victory over sin, over death, and over all things on the earth.

> *I have been crucified with Christ; it is no longer I who live, but Christ lives in me; and the life which I now live in the flesh I live by faith in the Son of God, who loved me and gave Himself for me.*
> —Galatians 2:20

The apostle Paul poured out his life for the sake of the gospel because of his intense gratitude for the gift of salvation. His was not a "take-it-or-leave-it" salvation. He didn't live for Christ only if others did or if no party was happening. It wasn't an optional lifestyle. He joined Christ in dedicating his entire life to sharing the gospel.

Probably no one who has ever lived has lived as intensely for Christ as Paul has, but what about you? Do you need to take your commitment to Christ up a notch?

THINK ABOUT IT

No doubt Paul felt he had been given much. What have you been given by Christ? Make a list of what Jesus Christ has done for you—He has forgiven you; blessed you; healed you; given you friends, family, health, potential, opportunity, a mind; and so on. List at least eight things.

> *For everyone to whom much is given, from him much will be required; and to whom much has been committed, of him they will ask the more.*
> —Luke 12:48

Study the gospel above: the death, burial, and resurrection of Christ (1 Corinthians 15:3–4). Commit to spending ten minutes each day studying the Scriptures and being able to thoroughly explain the gospel to others.

Paul, compelled by the love of Christ, urges you to hold tenaciously to these truths.

This gospel is the real deal.

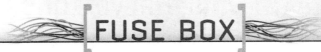

[FUSE BOX]

Make sure that what you are exposed to has passed the test on:

1. the divine person and work of Christ;
2. that He died for the sin of the world;
3. was buried and rose from the dead;
4. according to the final authority of the Holy Scriptures, the Word of God.

Faith is a living, daring confidence in God's grace, so sure and certain that a man could stake his life on it a thousand times.
—Martin Luther

PRIVATE WORLD DEVOTIONS

MONDAY: See it. Read the surrounding passages or chapter for the Key Scripture so that you can get an understanding of the background and context. This helps you to really *see* the verse.

TUESDAY: Hear it. Read the daily Key Scripture and/or surrounding passage out loud, putting your name in, if applicable. For example, <u>John</u> *can do all things through Christ. Thieves have come to destroy* <u>John</u>, *but Jesus has come that* <u>John</u> *might have eternal life.*

WEDNESDAY: Write it. Write the verse and then what it says about:

✦ *Others:* Respond, serve, and love as Jesus would.

✦ *Me:* Specific attitudes, choices, or habits.

✦ *God:* His love, mercy, holiness, peace, joy, etc.

PRIVATE WORLD JOURNAL

I am grateful for—I praise You for—I am feeling—I am thinking—I need help with

PRIVATE WORLD DEVOTIONS *(Continued)*

THURSDAY: Memorize it. Take the verse with you—write it on a card or put it in your phone, iPod, or PDA. Go over it throughout the day so that it begins to *live* in your heart and mind.

FRIDAY: Pray it. Personalize the verse as you pray for yourself or for others or in praise to God. To pray is literally "to think about." Try thinking out loud or writing in your **PRIVATE WORLD JOURNAL.**

SATURDAY: Share it. Ask the Lord to bring someone to mind or in your path today who needs good news. Don't be shy—just let it out! Whether you IM, write, text, tell, or send it, the joy of God's Word will flow from your heart into theirs.

PRAYER REQUESTS

Date	Name	Need	Answer

PRIVATE WORLD JOURNAL

I am grateful for—I praise You for—I am feeling—I am thinking—I need help with

NOTES

THE MEETING AHEAD, PART 1

KEY SCRIPTURE

Therefore we make it our aim, whether present or absent, to be well pleasing to Him. For we must all appear before the judgment seat of Christ, that each one may receive the things done in the body, according to what he has done, whether good or bad.

2 Corinthians 5:9–10

THIS REALLY HAPPENED!

Twelve-year-old Bobby had sat at his mother's bedside many times in the last year. He gave her water to sip, wiped her brow, and read to her. His mom had been sick for a long time, and his dad said that she was going soon to meet Jesus.

Bobby couldn't imagine a day without his mom, but he didn't want her to have pain or cry anymore. Over and over, he went to the Bible, to that verse that his mom told him about: "God will wipe away every tear from their eyes; there shall be no more death, nor sorrow, nor crying. There shall be no more pain, for the former things have passed away" (Revelation 21:4).

"Mama, are you afraid?" he would ask her.

"No, Bobby," she'd answer, "I'm not afraid. You see, I gave my life to Christ many years ago, and I know that Jesus has prepared a place for me."

Just a few days later, Bobby sat at his mom's side while she slept. Suddenly, she opened her eyes, smiled, and lifted up her hands toward heaven. Bobby knew Jesus had come to lead her to that prepared place where she would never hurt again.

WHY KNOW IT?

✦ 29% of non-Christians think they will go to heaven.[1]

✦ 76% of Americans believe in a heaven.[2]

✦ 75% believe their actions on earth will determine whether they go there.[3]

transfuse (trans FYOOZ): to cause to pass from one to another; transmit

The apostle Paul was one motivated guy, no doubt. His first thought, first breath, first action of the day was planned around telling the story of Jesus.

He faced persecutions;

humiliation on a daily basis;

financial destitution;

and a wicked and sinful culture.

Still, he kept going. Nothing got in his way; nothing detoured him from living for Christ.

We know that Paul's central motivation came from his own experience with Christ, the salvation that had so drastically changed him. But there was another thing he could not shake and he taught and spoke of it often—the meeting ahead.

There are two meetings ahead, one for the Christian and one for the person who does not believe in Christ. We will study both of these meetings, because both have a bearing on our motivation toward evangelism. Today's lesson, however, will focus on the judgment seat of Christ for Christians and the reward of heaven that follows.

Therefore we make it our aim, whether present or absent, to be well pleasing to Him. For we must all appear before the judgment seat of Christ, that each one may receive the things done in the body, according to what he has done, whether good or bad. —2 Corinthians 5:9–10

The Greek word we translate "judgment seat" (*bema*) basically means "step," and it was used as a unit of measure. The word *bema* is used to describe a raised platform on which a judge sat during judicial proceedings (and from which he pronounced his verdict) or of the seat itself.[4]

It is clear from this verse that every one of us must stand before Christ as an individual. At that time, we will not be able to hide anything or disguise ourselves. On this day, Christ will:

+ reveal what we have done and why we have done it;

+ reveal what we have not done and why we failed to do so;

+ hold us accountable for every day of our lives;

+ give us our subsequent rewards.

Now this is something you don't hear about every day! No one wants to imagine that every word, thought, and deed will be judged by Christ Himself, but it will happen. The understanding of this takes us immediately out of the moment and into living every day with the future in mind.

THINK ABOUT IT

If you knew that tomorrow you would be standing at the judgment seat of Christ, what would you have done differently this week?

_____

_____

_____

We have discussed judgment of motive, but let's now look at the rewards of that day. The greatest reward is to stand before Christ and know that we lived for Him. If that is the priority of our minds, then we will live for Him with our hearts. That is huge.

We will receive crowns, given to us as rewards, which we will then be able to lay at the feet of Jesus. It will be an incredible day as you present to Him the gift of your life's work.

Here are just a few of the crowns that the Bible talks about:

✦ Crown of Endurance (James 1:12)

✦ Crown of Righteousness (2 Timothy 4:8)

✦ Crown of the Martyr (Revelation 2:10)

All three of these crowns have to do with our attitude and behavior.

Do you think that Jesus chose these crowns because He understands the temptations and struggles you are going through?

THE MEETING AHEAD, PART 1

diffuse (di FYOOZ) : to pour out and permit or cause to spread freely; to extend, scatter

The two crowns we want to study today are the crowns of spiritual leadership and personal evangelism.

Crown of Spiritual Leadership

> Shepherd the flock of God which is among you
> . . . not by compulsion but willingly, not for
> dishonest gain but eagerly, nor as being lords
> over those entrusted to you, but being examples
> to the flock; and when the Chief Shepherd
> appears, you will receive the crown of glory
> that does not fade away. —**1 Peter 5:2–4**

Each of you who knows Christ personally can be an example to other Christians in your youth group. The church, ordained by Christ, loved by Christ, is the place where you can serve. It begins with your example and encouragement to other believers.

For each person that you minister to within your church, your influence is multiplied. That's God's plan—you help one who helps another, who encourages another, who reaches another, and so on.

THINK ABOUT IT

Think about your role as a leader in your youth group. What does it mean to be a spiritual leader?

List ONE THING you can do this week to show spiritual leadership in your youth group and/or at your school.

Can you think of ONE PERSON you might be able to encourage this week or even today?

What would you say?

What Scripture could you give him or her for the situation?

Crown of Personal Evangelism

For what is our hope, or joy, or crown of rejoicing? Is it not even you in the presence of our Lord Jesus Christ at His coming? For you are our glory and joy. —**1 Thessalonians 2:19–20**

Imagine . . . You are standing in front of Christ, awaiting your life to be shown on the big screen. You look around and see the one who sat beside you on the bleachers, the one you met at a party, the one you got to know through football camp, and the one who sang with you at choir.

You realize, "I had a part in them standing here, in front of Christ." What an incredible thought! Paul must have had these kinds of thoughts often for he talked over and over of those he loved dearly, those whom he shared the gospel of Christ with who were now serving in churches around the world.

THINK ABOUT IT

The judgment seat of Christ occurs at the end of time. Why? Because your influence, or the lack of it, goes on and on and on throughout generations until the end of time.

Facts About Heaven

- It is a "holy city" called "the New Jerusalem" (Revelation 21:2).

- It is 1,500 miles square, with a highest point of 1,500 miles and walls made of jasper stone, measuring 216 feet in height (Revelation 21:16–18).

- The foundations of this beautiful city bear the names of the twelve apostles and are decorated with precious stones. Each of the twelve gates (three in each of the four walls) will carry the name of one of the twelve tribes of Israel, and each gate is made of a single pearl (Revelation 21:12–13, 21).

- The street of the city is gold so pure that it is clear (Revelation 21:21).

- Flowing from the throne of God is a crystal-clear river of the water of life, and on either side is planted the tree of life, bearing twelve types of fruit every month (Revelation 22:1–3).

GROUP DISCUSSION

Get out your "I Believe in Prayer" Journal and spend several minutes as a group, each person praying silently for a person on his or her list.

What Is Heaven Like?
For the one who has received Christ personally, there is a prepared place called heaven.

Why would we even want to go there?

✦ *There is a place prepared for you.* Jesus said, "In My Father's house are many mansions; if it were not so, I would have told you. I go to prepare a place for you" (John 14:2).

✦ *Jesus is there.* Paul said that God raised Christ from the dead and "seated Him at His right hand in the heavenly places" (Ephesians 1:20).

✦ *Jesus is waiting to receive us.* He said, "I will come again and receive you to Myself; that where I am, there you may be also" (John 14:3).

What determines whether a person is accepted into heaven? Let's ask the One who prepares heaven for us, Jesus.

Jesus gave us the requirement for entering heaven. "Most assuredly, I say to you, unless one is born again, he cannot see the kingdom of God" (John 3:3).

What Is Heaven Missing?
In heaven, there will be no more:

✦ hunger or thirst (Revelation 7:16)

✦ tears (Revelation 21:4)

✦ night (Revelation 21:25)

✦ sin or consequence of sin (Revelation 21:27)

✦ Anyone whose name is not written in the Book of Life (Revelation 21:27)

How Can You Be Sure You Will Go to Heaven?

Jesus answered and said to him, "Most assuredly, I say to you, unless one is born again, he cannot see the kingdom of God." **—John 3:3**

If you confess with your mouth the Lord Jesus and believe in your heart that God has raised Him from the dead, you will be saved. For with the heart one believes unto righteousness, and with the mouth confession is made unto salvation. **—Romans 10:9–10**

[FUSE BOX]

Heaven is indeed a real, magnificent place. No wonder Paul reminded us that "to die is gain" (Philippians 1:21).
Will you be there? Will your friends be there?

There are only two days that matter: Today and *that* day [speaking of the judgment].
—Martin Luther

PRIVATE WORLD DEVOTIONS

MONDAY: See it. Read the surrounding passages or chapter for the Key Scripture so that you can get an understanding of the background and context. This helps you to really *see* the verse.

TUESDAY: Hear it. Read the daily Key Scripture and/or surrounding passage out loud, putting your name in, if applicable. For example, <u>John</u> *can do all things through Christ. Thieves have come to destroy* <u>John</u>, *but Jesus has come that* <u>John</u> *might have eternal life.*

WEDNESDAY: Write it. Write the verse and then what it says about:

✦ *Others:* Respond, serve, and love as Jesus would.

✦ *Me:* Specific attitudes, choices, or habits.

✦ *God:* His love, mercy, holiness, peace, joy, etc.

PRIVATE WORLD JOURNAL

I am grateful for—I praise You for—I am feeling—I am thinking—I need help with

PRIVATE WORLD DEVOTIONS *(Continued)*

THURSDAY: Memorize it. Take the verse with you—write it on a card or put it in your phone, iPod, or PDA. Go over it throughout the day so that it begins to *live* in your heart and mind.

FRIDAY: Pray it. Personalize the verse as you pray for yourself or for others or in praise to God. To pray is literally "to think about." Try thinking out loud or writing in your **PRIVATE WORLD JOURNAL**.

SATURDAY: Share it. Ask the Lord to bring someone to mind or in your path today who needs good news. Don't be shy—just let it out! Whether you IM, write, text, tell, or send it, the joy of God's Word will flow from your heart into theirs.

PRAYER REQUESTS

Date	Name	Need	Answer

PRIVATE WORLD JOURNAL

I am grateful for—I praise You for—I am feeling—I am thinking—I need help with

NOTES

CHAPTER 8

THE MEETING AHEAD, PART 2

KEY SCRIPTURE

But I say to you that for every idle word men may speak, they will give account of it in the day of judgment.

Matthew 12:36

THIS REALLY HAPPENED!

Sarah wanted nothing to do with God. Her mother died when she was just five, and she blamed God. She felt so angry and alone. Friends talked to her about God's love and invited her to church, but she replied with foul language, "Leave me alone."

One friend, Kayce, kept on reaching out even when Sarah was rude. "I am praying for you," she said. "I want you to know how much God loves you. And I care about you as a friend."

Just a few days later, Sarah was in a horrific car accident. Her back was broken, and she hovered between life and death for two days. When she finally opened her eyes, the first person she saw was Kayce smiling down at her. "Hi, girl, I've been praying for you."

Sarah couldn't move any part of her body, but that didn't stop the tears from flowing down her face. Suddenly all the anger didn't matter. God loved her—she knew that now. And Kayce had shown that love through her friendship.

Sarah thought about the prayer of salvation that she had heard Kayce tell her about so many times. She thought about how close she had come to death and the anger she was holding on to. At that moment, Sarah closed her eyes and opened her heart to Christ. The tears still flowed, but now they were tears of joy.

WHY KNOW IT?

✦ 68% of people believe in the devil[1]

✦ Nearly 2/3 of people think they're going to heaven, while few believe they're hell-bound[2]

transfuse (trans FYOOZ)́: to cause to pass from one
to another; transmit

In the previous chapter, we saw that the apostle Paul was motivated by the judgment seat of Christ, where his works would be judged and rewarded before he entered heaven. But there was another day, a terrible day, that haunted him day and night: the final judgment day of the unbeliever.

Throughout the Bible, we are told that people are accountable to God. Good deeds are commended and evil deeds are blamed. The day of judgment is the culmination of the whole process. At the end of this world order God will judge all people and all deeds. Nothing will be excepted; every secret thing, good or bad, will be brought into judgment.[3]

Far be it from You to do such a thing as this,
to slay the righteous with the wicked, so
that the righteous should be as the wicked;
far be it from You! Shall not the Judge of
all the earth do right? —**Genesis 18:25**

God appears throughout the Old Testament in the role of "Judge of all the earth" or as the God of justice. The spotlight of the New Testament falls on the future and final event of judgment that will accompany the return of Christ. This has often been called the Great White Throne Judgment. It is the last and final judgment of the man or woman who has died without Christ.

1. Christ Himself will be the Judge (2 Timothy 4:1).

2. All men will be judged and none will escape (1 Peter 4:5).

3. Even the angels will be judged (2 Peter 2:4; Jude 6).

4. The purposes of the heart will be revealed (1 Corinthians 4:5).

5. Every careless word will be revealed (Matthew 12:36).

6. Every aspect of life will be revealed (Romans 2:16).

7. Death and judgment are appointed for all mankind (Hebrews 9:27).

Why are there two different judgments? Because each has a specific purpose for a specific outcome.

infuse (in FYOOZ); to cause to be permeated with something (as a principle or quality) that alters usually for the better

In this study guide, we have studied Paul's life as the model Christian. He has been given the highest honor of a Christian—that is, an ambassador of God Himself. Charged with sharing the amazing message of salvation with all of mankind, he proclaims to the highest authority and to the lowest slave that mercy, forgiveness, and grace are found through the cross.

Wow! That's pretty amazing stuff.

On the other hand, Paul is subject to every kind of human weakness and frailty. Most biographers believe he had weak vision, was not physically attractive, and had poor health. Add to this the persecutions and sufferings we have already discussed that he endured for the gospel's sake.

How did he endure? Paul kept his eye on the future, not on the pain of the present. The future, with all of its glorious certainty, eclipsed any sufferings and disappointments that the present held. That is why he wrote: "For I consider that the sufferings of this present time are not worthy to be compared with the glory which shall be revealed in us" (Romans 8:18).

What's troubling you about the upcoming week? Tests, stress of too much to do—homework, sports, family, problem in a relationship, illness you must deal with, family financial burdens? All of these are very, very real and cause debilitating distress. How can you use Paul's principle of Romans 8:18 to deal with your life?

Problem:

_____

_____

_____

_____

> Weigh the cost of discipleship against the eternal weight of glory, and you will have the true balance of things.

Paul's corresponding problem:

_____

_____

_____

_____

What eternity holds for you: (refer to last week's lesson)

_____

_____

_____

_____

We have talked about the glory of heaven, but it must be asked, "Is there really a hell?" After all, we don't hear much about it anymore. Maybe it was just an "old-time preacher" thing.

Or maybe it is a Jesus thing.

Jesus, the most compassionate, caring Person who ever lived, taught the reality of hell and spoke more of hell than He did about heaven. In the Sermon on the Mount alone, He warned His followers over a half dozen times.

If Jesus was compassionate for others yet didn't shy away from warning them about hell, what does that mean for you? Are you avoiding telling your friends about hell because you think that's not a "loving" thing to do? If so, think about this. Which action is truly more loving and compassionate: to warn your friends about the danger of eternal suffering, or to avoid hurting their feelings by not saying anything?

GROUP DISCUSSION

If we are to tell others of the intense love of Christ, how can we bring up hell? Isn't that a contradiction?

- ✦ It is because God loves us so much that He warns of the reality of hell, the place created for the devil and his angels.

- ✦ It is because of hell that Jesus suffered, bled, and died.

- ✦ Jesus rose from the dead to show that hell holds no power over the one who believes in Christ.

- ✦ Every person has the power to avoid hell by accepting Christ's gift of salvation.

What is ONE THING you can be prepared to discuss about hell that will show how easy it is for every person to miss?

_____

_____

_____

What Is Hades?

In Luke 16:19–31, Jesus described in detail a place called Hades. There are those who refer to this passage as a parable rather than a true story. However, Jesus never used proper names in parables, as He did in Luke 16, thus proving its accuracy as a true story.

Luke 16 describes Hades like the local city jail—a place where prisoners are kept until their trial. When one dies without Christ, the body is buried, but the spirit goes immediately to Hades. The Christian, on the other hand, also is buried, but is immediately brought into the presence of God.

What Is Hades Like?

Several facts are known about Hades:

+ *Man is conscious in Hades.* The rich man felt pain, saw Abraham and Lazarus (Luke 16:23), and spoke to Abraham (Luke 16:22, 24) and was thirsty (Luke 16:24).

+ *Man has a memory in Hades.* Abraham asked the rich man to remember his life and the way he had chosen to live. At this suggestion the rich man also remembered his five brothers and begged Abraham to send a warning to them about the torments of Hades (Luke 16:25–28). The unbeliever will remember all the times he might have said yes to God.

✦ *Man finds no escape from Hades.* The rich man begged for water, but Abraham was unable to accommodate him. Abraham spoke of a great gulf that separated them. No one was able to pass between the two places (Luke 16:26).

What Is Hell?

The Greek word *gehenna*, translated "hell," appears twelve times in the Greek New Testament. Eleven of those times it is used by Jesus Himself. *Gehenna* is the final punishment. This can be compared to the federal penitentiary, the next step after the local jail.

What Is Hell Like?

Several descriptions are given about hell:

✦ Lake of fire and brimstone (Revelation 20:10, 14, 15)

✦ Fire that shall never be quenched (Mark 9:43)

✦ Everlasting fire (Matthew 18:8–9; 25:41)

✦ Outer darkness (Matthew 8:12; 22:13; 25:30)

✦ Everlasting punishment (Matthew 25:46)

✦ Weeping and gnashing of teeth (Matthew 25:30)

Two of the world's greatest artists have rendered amazing works of the horrors of hell. Rodin's *Gates of Hell* in Paris and Michelangelo's *Last Judgment* at the Sistine Chapel seem to say to the viewer, "Prepare to meet God." As incredible and detailed as these works are, they are not the compelling evidences of the consequences of a lost soul. The most persuasive argument is the life and teachings of Jesus Himself.

diffuse (di FYOOZ) ; to pour out and permit or cause to spread freely; to extend, scatter

Is Hell a Real Place?

While the doctrine of eternal punishment is not very popular, it is a major teaching of the Bible. Why do you think that a majority of people don't believe in hell?

Do you think it is because:

✦ They don't want to?

✦ They think of themselves as good people?

✦ They believe hell is reserved for terrorists, murders, and *major* sinners?

✦ What else?

Why do you think we rarely discuss hell?

THINK ABOUT IT:

Without the reality of hell:

✦ there would be no need for a Savior or for the cross.

✦ the suffering of Christ on the cross would have been for nothing.

 When you share the gospel, be sure to focus on three things:

✦ *God's love for you*—He has a unique purpose and plan for your life.

✦ *God's love for you*—He wants you to be with Him for all of eternity in a place called heaven.

✦ *God's love for you*—He died for you so that you would never have to experience the reality of hell.

Be ready to share the gospel with someone this week!

To die without Jesus is very serious.

Don't be fooled into thinking that:

✦ the believer will live in mansions while unbelievers live in the ghetto;

✦ that the believer rides first-class while the unbeliever flies on the single-engine plane; in fact, we are not even on the same plane.

Do You *Really* Believe in Hell?

When we look into our hearts and get real with ourselves, we must admit that most Christians don't really believe in the reality of hell.

Yes? We do? Then how do you explain our silence and our lack of tears for those who are without Christ?

At the final day of judgment, the unbeliever will be alone. There will no crowd to blame problems on, no parents to speak up in his defense. He will not be questioned about the sins of his friends or classmates, nor about the mistakes of his parents. His life—and his alone—will be on trial, and the determining factor will be what decision he made about Christ and the gift of eternal life He purchased and offered.

At that time, the Bible tells us, "Anyone not found written in the Book of Life was cast into the lake of fire" (Revelation 20:15).

Now, if you get nothing else we have studied so far, you must get this:

- ✦ Death brings judgment and hell for the non-Christian.

- ✦ Death brings eternal, joyful communion with God for the Christian.

These thoughts should motivate us to communicate the good news of salvation to everyone. They also serve as a warning to examine ourselves as to whether we truly have been born again, lest we be like the rich man in Luke 16 who decided to pray for mercy and forgiveness, but only after it was too late.

Who will you witness to this week?

_____

_____

_____

Do you know how to intelligently present the good news?

_____

_____

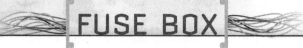

[FUSE BOX]

When we know the Word of God as truth,
we are able to confidently share our faith
with others. When we live the Word of God
as truth, our first thoughts and actions are to
love and serve unconditionally.

NOTES

"It's only good news
if they hear it in
time."
—David Burton

PRIVATE WORLD DEVOTIONS

MONDAY: See it. Read the surrounding passages or chapter for the Key Scripture so that you can get an understanding of the background and context. This helps you to really *see* the verse.

TUESDAY: Hear it. Read the daily Key Scripture and/or surrounding passage out loud, putting your name in, if applicable. For example, <u>John</u> *can do all things through Christ. Thieves have come to destroy* <u>John</u>*, but Jesus has come that* <u>John</u> *might have eternal life.*

WEDNESDAY: Write it. Write the verse and then what it says about:

- ✦ *Others:* Respond, serve, and love as Jesus would.
- ✦ *Me:* Specific attitudes, choices, or habits.
- ✦ *God:* His love, mercy, holiness, peace, joy, etc.

PRIVATE WORLD JOURNAL

I am grateful for—I praise You for—I am feeling—I am thinking—I need help with

PRIVATE WORLD DEVOTIONS (Continued)

THURSDAY: Memorize it. Take the verse with you—write it on a card or put it in your phone, iPod, or PDA. Go over it throughout the day so that it begins to *live* in your heart and mind.

FRIDAY: Pray it. Personalize the verse as you pray for yourself or for others or in praise to God. To pray is literally "to think about." Try thinking out loud or writing in your **PRIVATE WORLD JOURNAL**.

SATURDAY: Share it. Ask the Lord to bring someone to mind or in your path today who needs good news. Don't be shy—just let it out! Whether you IM, write, text, tell, or send it, the joy of God's Word will flow from your heart into theirs.

PRAYER REQUESTS

Date	Name	Need	Answer

PRIVATE WORLD JOURNAL

I am grateful for—I praise You for—I am feeling—I am thinking—I need help with

NOTES

"I BELIEVE IN PRAYER" JOURNAL

Name

Personal Need

Action (i.e., write a note, share a verse, call to say hello, introduce to a friend, invite to an event, etc.)

Step

Name

Personal Need

Action (i.e., write a note, share a verse, call to say hello, introduce to a friend, invite to an event, etc.)

Step

Name

Personal Need

Action (i.e., write a note, share a verse, call to say hello, introduce to a friend, invite to an event, etc.)

Step

Notes

CHAPTER 1: IT STARTS WITH YOU!

1. The Barna Group, "Evangelism" (2004). http://www.barna.org/FlexPage.aspx?Page = Topic&TopicID = 18 (accessed 24 November 2005).

2. Ibid.

CHAPTER 2: THE MANDATE FROM ABOVE

1. U.S. Department of Education, "Religious Expression in Public Schools" (1998 May). http://www.ed.gov/Speeches/08-1995/religion.html (accessed 18 July 2005).

2. Ibid.

3. Ibid.

4. Ibid.

5. Ibid.

6. U.S. Department of Education, "The Equal Access Act" (1998 May). http://www.ed.gov/Speeches/08-1995/religion.html (accessed 18 July 2005).

7. Kenneth S. Wuest, *Wuest's Word Studies from the Greek New Testament,* vol. 3 (Grand Rapids: Eerdmans, 1973), s.v. "bond-servant."

CHAPTER 3: MIRACLE WITHIN

1. The Barna Group, "Teenagers," (2004). http://www.barna.org/FlexPage.aspx?Page = Topic&TopicID = 37 (accessed 24 November 2005).

2. Ibid.

CHAPTER 4: MOTIVATED BY THE MULTITUDES

1. The Barna Group, "Evangelism" (2004). http://www.barna.org/ FlexPage.aspx?Page = Topic&TopicID = 18 (accessed 24 November 2005).

2. Ibid.

3. Ibid.

4. Charles Ferguson Ball, *The Life and Times of the Apostle Paul* (Wheaton, Ill.: Tyndale, 1996), 6.

CHAPTER 5: PRAYING FOR THE LOST

1. Cult Hotline and Clinic, "Cult Statistics." http://www.cultclinic. org/qa2.html (accessed 24 November 2005).

2. David Barrett, et al., *World Christian Encyclopedia: A Comparative Survey of Churches and Religions—AD 30 to 2200* (New York: Oxford University Press, 2001).

CHAPTER 7: THE MEETING AHEAD, PART 1

1. Humphrey Taylor, "The Religious and Other Beliefs of Americans 2003," Harris Interactive, Inc. (26 February 2003). http://www. harrisinteractive.com/harris_poll/index.asp?PID = 359 (accessed 24 November 2005).

2. Ted Olsen, "What Percentage of Americans Believe in Heaven?" *Christianity Today, September 9, 2002.*

3. Ibid.

4. Walter A. Elwell, ed., Baker's Evangelical Dictionary of Biblical Theology (Grand Rapids: Baker, 1996), s.v. "Judgment Seat of Christ."

CHAPTER 8: THE MEETING AHEAD, PART 2

1. Humphrey Taylor, "The Religious and Other Beliefs of Americans 2003," Harris Interactive, Inc. (26 February 2003). http://www. harrisinteractive.com/harris_poll/index.asp?PID = 359 (accessed 24 November 2005).

2. K. Connie Kang, "Next Stop, the Pearly Gates . . . or Hell?" *Los Angeles Times,* www.forf.org/news/2004/heavenorhell.html (accessed 24 November 2005).

3. Walter A. Elwell, ed., Baker's Evangelical Dictionary of Biblical Theology (Grand Rapids: Baker, 1996), s.v. "Day of Judgment."

ABOUT THE AUTHOR

Jay Strack, president and founder of Student Leadership University, is an inspiring and effective communicator, author, and minister. Acclaimed by leaders in the business world, religious affiliations, and education realms as a dynamic speaker, Jay has spoken to an estimated 15 million people in his 30 years of ministry. His versatile style has been presented across the United States and in 22 other countries, before government officials, corporate groups, numerous professional sports teams in the NFL, NBA, and MLB, to over 9,500 school assemblies, and at some 100 universities. Zig Ziglar calls Jay Strack, "entertaining, but powerful, inspiring and informative."

Leadership with a twist.

SLU Xtreme and Creative Outbreak Workshop

Student Leadership University understands that every leader is unique. That's why we've created two new programs: **C**reative **O**utbreak **W**orkshop and SLU Extreme.

COW - *Whether behind the camera or in front, you'll learn the latest in technique and technology from the nation's best. Add in leadership, SLU style, and you'll find yourself empowered to stand strong in the entertainment industry.*

SLU Extreme – *Here's your chance to try on extreme sports while learning how to lead and influence others.*

SLU – come for the original or try the extra spicy! We give you the adventure of a lifetime.

For more information call
Toll-free: 1-888-260-2900
www.studentleadership.net

Student Leadership
UNIVERSITY

Lead, follow or be bait.

This is where the journey begins – SLU101!

At Student Leadership University, you won't find canoes and campfires. What you will find is a 4-day comprehensive program designed to catapult you into a life of confidence, significance, and leadership. SLU prepares you to successfully navigate the shark-infested waters of our culture with the rules and tools of leadership. Stop hanging out with the bait fish. Come to SLU where dreaming is encouraged and the language of leadership is spoken freely.

Explore the possibilities at
www.studentleadership.net

Student Leadership
UNIVERSITY

The journey continues.
SLU201, SLU301, SLU401! – We kick it up a notch!
Student Leadership University believes you'll be the same person five years from now as you are today, except for...The places you go,The people you meet, The books you read. 201-Washington, D.C. – Exclusive SLU 201 Level Two Sessions in Leadership, Worldview, and Behind the Scenes experiences give an in-depth look at the foundation of our country. 301-London-Paris-Normandy-Oxford – Step off the plane and into history as we honor the past and learn to transform the future. 401-Rome-Athens-Ephesus-Florence-Pompeii – Explorethe days of ancient history and get inspired to Live a Legacy of Faith.
For more information call
Toll-free: 1-888-260-2900
www.studentleadership.net
Student Leadership University